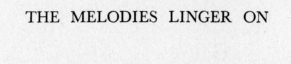

THE MELODIES LINGER ON

Other C. H. books by Larry Freeman

Cavalcade of Toys
Child's Picture Book
The Merry Old Mobiles
One Collector's Luck
Light On Old Lamps
Nursery Americana
Early American Silver
China Classics
Antique Furniture I
How to Price Antiques
Blue Book Musical Shows

THE
Melodies
Linger On

50 YEARS OF POPULAR SONG

=

By Larry Freeman

Century House, Watkins Glen, N.Y.

A Prefatory Note . . .

AMERICANS HAVE ALWAYS LOVED TO SING, always had a keen ear for melody. Our folk songs are built on the best from many lands. The early colonists sang in praise and thanksgiving. Westward with course of empire went Stephen Foster's *Oh, Susannah* and many another 19th century hit. Just as surely do the songs of the last fifty years mark the interests and progress of a great nation; the ethics, habits and intimate life of its people. From *Sweet Adeline* to *White Christmas*, the 20th century has given us songs that will live forever. To recall their lure and lore is the purpose of this book.

This is a book about songs, not a song book. The song covers and advertisements which make up most of the pages are intended primarily to jog the memory and whet the imagination. From literally hundreds of sources have come these mementoes of the near-past. Hidden in piles of attic trash or laying forgotten in old music cabinets, the original issues of our most popular 'popular songs' are particularly difficult to come upon. Nor is it easy to find the cover or theatrical advertisement associated with the star-personality who helped put a given song across. By its very nature, the popular song sheet has a short life. It is bought today and burned to-morrow. The author is grateful to all who helped unearth such ephemera, and thanks especially the publishers and agencies for use of much old-time material. Certain reproduction courtesies have been handled by credit lines under the pictures used. Many original song publishers are now out of business. But wherever possible the present copyright holders are given in connection with the fifty year list of song hits posted at the end of the book.

As the staggering amount of research that goes into projects of this kind got under way, it became obvious that there wasn't room for everything. But if some favorite song title has been left out, others of similar nature will be found included.

No attempt will be made to list the individuals who helped put together the materials which make up this book. From start to finish, it has been a matter of enthusiastic experimentation by many hands.

The idea of trying to elicit tomal memories by pictorial cue dictated a unique format. Text had to be set in conformity with each picture used; only where a few odd lines were needed to complete a page layout could the author digress to more general matters. Continuity is supplied, however, by brief essays at the beginning and end of each decade of song. These show how the instruments used in popularizing song have changed with the times. In 1900 we have the singing voice in CLOSE HARMONY. 1910 gives us PIANO ACCOMPANIMENT. In 1920 we have PHONOGRAPH FEVER, in 1930, MUSIC IN THE AIR, in 1940, JUKE BOX JAMBOREE. 1950 brings us to the end of our story, reviews the CONTINUED PERFORMANCE of love songs. A listing, by years, of the hit tunes of the past half century is also appended.

This is in no sense a scholarly book. It aspires to no great pronouncements on the future of popular song. Its comments on the past are nostalgic rather than critical. Though the popular song is a revealing index of American life in general, and of American musical taste in particular, the record has been left largely to speak for itself.

Only in his capacity as a psychologist does the author inject a personal viewpoint. Here he protests the growing tendency to spectator rather than participant activity in song. Today it is easiest to watch someone else play your baseball and to listen to someone else sing your songs. But those who want to get the most good out of their leisure time will play and sing along with the professionals! It is hoped this book will revive in people the memories of melodies they used to know, help restore the almost lost art of singing for pleasure alone. If the ephemera of popular song here collected have any historical value, let that be incidental.

LARRY FREEMAN

Freeman Farms,
Watkins Glen, N. Y.
October 15, 1950

1900

Close Harmony . . .

NO ONE KNOWS quite when the 'popular song' first hit the American public squarely between its ears. In the latter part of the 19th Century touring minstrel shows and the growing vaudeville circuit were carrying catchy new tunes well into the hinterland. People everywhere had begun to sing and hum the melodies that were introduced on the stage, at political rallys and ball games, in department stores,—in fact, anywhere that folks congregated. By 1900 (again apeing the professionals) they were, in duos and quartets, such old hits as *Sweet Rosie O'Grady*, *After the Ball* and *Break the News to Mother*. The stage had been set for that all-time barbershop favorite, *Sweet Adeline* (1903). It was the era of CLOSE HARMONY.

Songs in those days, much more than now, owed their popularization to the personal performance of their writer-composers. It is highly significant that men like George M. Cohan, Gus Edwards, the Von Tilzer's, even Victor Herbert, were showmen first and song writers by necessity. In order to make their vaudeville acts and stage shows continue to draw crowds, they would often compose topical songs or on-the-spot ballads of sure-fire appeal. No closeting of self away from the public eye for these stalwarts; they maintained intimate contact with the people, and most of their songs were of the people! Singability rather than instrumental accompaniment was the hallmark of a song's success. Whether performed by amateur or professional, for pleasure or for profit, emphasis was laid on a simple melody (within an octave range), with a long holding of the last full chord. Attention was also paid to the story-telling quality of the words. *After the Ball* and many another song whose cover is shown on the pages which follow, set a pattern of widespread appeal. And while it soon became the fashion to spoof the sentimental ballad, singing America must acknowledge its debt; *After the Ball* was originally performed in full evening dress by the ace song-plugger of his day. Few moderns can understand why this particular combination of words and music could have so completely upset singing America. It achieved an all-time record of 4,000,-000 copies sold. Today, a 100,000 copy sale is bonanza in sheet music.

AFTER THE BALL

...As...
Sung by
J. Aldrich
Libbey
...the...
Peerless Baritone
in HOYT'S
"A Trip to
Chinatown"

-- BY --
Chas. K. Harris

J. Aldrich Libbey, the Peerless Baritone

Published by CHAS. K. HARRIS, Milwaukee, Wis.

AFTER THE BALL (1892) set the pattern for whole cycle of doleful recitatives, was often presented to audiences with accompanying lantern slides. This type of ballad was being parodied thus in 1900:

After the ball is over, Mary takes out her glass eye
Puts her false teeth in cold water, corks up her bottle of dye
Throws her cork leg in the corner, hangs up her wig on the wall:
Then what is left goes to bylo , AFTER THE BALL.

BARBER SHOP FAVORITES. Besides the above, we might mention *In The Shade Of The Old Apple Tree*, *Banks Of The Wabash*, many another period piece. *Sweet Adeline* was so named because its authors needed something to rhyme with "for you I pine", and bethought themselves of Adeline Patti, then making her farewell tour of America. Introduced by such professionals as the Quaker City Four, it was quickly taken up by amateur barber-shop quartets, with a long holding of the last full chord. *On the Banks of the Wabash*, by Paul Dresser, has been made the Indiana state song. *In the Shade of the Old Apple Tree*, by Van Alystyne, typifies the nostalgic yearning that city-country boys have for the home place. *Down By The Old Mill Stream* is a one song hit; its composer was never heard from thereafter. *Barber Shop Chord* is a novelty number, introduced in an early Follies show. *Dear Old Girl* is the composers' memorial to his wife. Forgotten today are the early barber shops that sang these songs, their rows of moustache cups and their two-bit haircuts. Only the beloved melodies live on in memory, heavy with the fragrance of simpler, carefree days . . .

"Dear . . . . Old . . . . Girl—Dear . . . . Old . . . . Girl—the robins sing above you . . . . it speaks of how I love you. Let the reader continue with his own Barber Shop Favorite.

CLOSE HARMONY received an ample supply of material from the sentimental balladry of this decade. *Sweet Adeline*, universal favorite of foursomes, dates from 1906.

REGINALD de KOVEN wrote music for 20 Broadway shows between 1890 and 1910; But Only this song, bids fare to pass into immortal fame. How many knew it came from operetta, ROBIN HOOD.

[14]

IN PRINCE OF PILZEN, Heidelburg Stein Song set pattern for many later versions of rollicking student drinking song.

Miss Trixie Friganza, favorite widow in PRINCE OF PILZEN, here shown in costume calculated to reveal her charms.

RARE SONG COVER. Though sold by the millions, who has this now?

GUS EDWARDS deserves a double niche in Tin Pan Alley's Hall of Fame. Not only was he a composer of 1,000,000 copy hits like the above; a vaudeville artist himself, he also discovered and developed a galaxy of top juvenile performers in his yearly song revues. Today, their names are written big in show business. Such proteges as George Jessel, Eddie Cantor (rescued from a knife-throwing act), Walter Winchell, Groucho Marx, Ray Bolger, Hildegarde, May Murray, Jack Pearl, The Duncan Sisters, Ann Dvorak and Sally Rand give truth to the 1939 movie title of Edwards life, THE STAR MAKER. Gus never had any children of his own, but during his lifetime he discovered scores and boys and girls and helped them on the way to stardom. The first Gus.Edwards School for Boys and Girls was in 1906. By 1910 he had his kids in the biggest vaudeville production ever attempted. This was the Gus Edwards' Song Revue. On the cover shown above he appears as a leader of newsboys, singing "*If I was a Millionaire.* Several famous stars can find themselves there also. But long after this Pied Piper and his original cast of stage struck children are forgotten, people will probably still be singing; "School Days, School Days, Dear Old Golden Rule Days. . . . When you wrote on my slate—I LOVE you Joe, when we were a couple of kids."

[17]

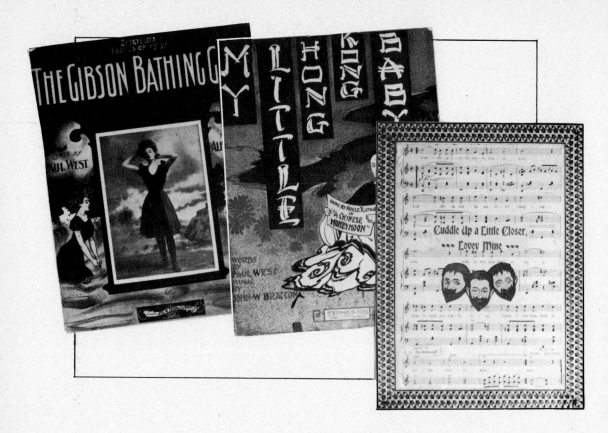

PACED BY the coon songs, the straight love ballad was losing much of its maudlin sentimentality and emerging in less inhibited dress. Here are three hot, business-like tunes that wowed them back in 1907. Only one is sufficiently up to date to be sung today. Sharp oldsters may remember *Come Be My Little Cup of Tea*, or the bathing beauty chorus of Ziegfeld's first Follies singing, *Mr. Gibson? Mr. Gibson? Can't We Go In To Swim*. Both were just as lilting waltz tunes as *Cuddle Up a Little Closer*.

If you went to dancing school in those days, the rule was two inches between the lady and her escort, and many chaperones wished to revive the schottish so as to combat the moral shortcomings of the new Viennese waltzes. You signed on the dotted line to dance with your friends out-of-town guest and you stayed with her to the bitter end. One did not 'cut in' in those days; it would have meant a fist fight out in the hall. If pretty but bored, you might beguile her by humming *I Wonder Who's Kissing Her Now* and see if you could get off her absentee list; if she was pretty and interested, you corresponded; if she was neither, songs like the above probably provide innumerable memories of girls you might have married.

[18]

A Scene from the 20th Century - Fox Production
"MY GAL SAL"

MY GAL SAL, the song and Victor Mature's movie of the composer's robust life, have both left their mark in Melody Lane. Composer Dresser's background for song writing was medicine tent shows.

[19]

FIVE GREAT STAGE SONGS. Lew Dockstader and his minstrel troupe will ever be remembered for songs like *Everybody Works But Father*. Comic Joe Weber had his own music hall, where he presented such robust parodies as *Hip, Hip, Hooray* . . . "A college yell in two shouts." Such shows, together with the Weberfieldian type of burlesque, have been sometimes likened to Gilbert and Sullivan operas. This can hardly be; themes here are more trivial, the words hardly up to Gilbert's nimble lyrics. American musical shows tended to excell in tuneful individual numbers. Songs like *Meet Me In St. Louis*, *In The Shade Of The Old Apple Tree* and *Shine On Harvest Moon* were interpolated in a number of stage revues.

[20]

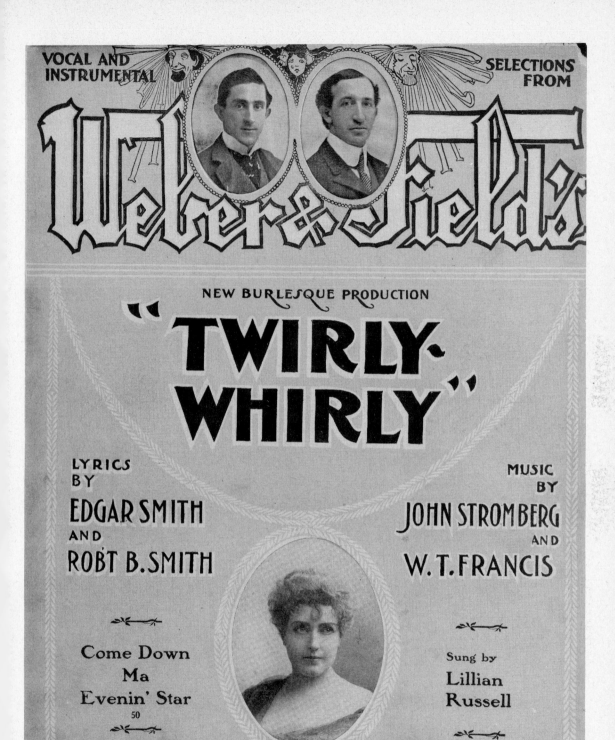

VOCAL AND INSTRUMENTAL

SELECTIONS FROM

Weber & Fields

NEW BURLESQUE PRODUCTION

"TWIRLY-WHIRLY"

LYRICS BY
EDGAR SMITH
AND
ROBT B. SMITH

MUSIC BY
JOHN STROMBERG
AND
W. T. FRANCIS

Come Down
Ma
Evenin' Star
50

Sung by
Lillian
Russell

LYRICAL BURLESQUES were Weber and Field's special domain, and Lillian Russell was the star in their crown. *Come Down My Evening Star*, found in John Stromberg's pocket at time of his death, was dedicated to her. Miss Russell broke down first time she sang it.

[21]

C L O R I N D Y

CAKE WALK

THE CAKE WALK. You who are over forty saw your first cake-walk in vaudeville: you who are under that age at a benefit show given by the men's club of the Lakewood Avenue Church. Sedate Caucasians never danced this high stepping, skirt-lifting walk, that is, if they wished to be classed as respectable. They got their exhileration second-hand by watching men in blackface 'carry on' with high-yellar girls. Above is the original cake walk, CLORINDY, by W. M. Cook.

Have yo' heard a-bout dat bul-ly dat's just come to town? He's
round a-mong de ——gers a-lay-in' their bod-ies down, I'm a-
—— ust be found.—— I'm a
—— n't al-low, No——
—— o raise a row. I'm——
look —— him bow.——
When I —— round, round, round, round,

STAGE MOTHER of ragtime was May Irwin, and the song that
put it over was called *The New Bully*. Originating in a colored bor-
dello, this type of 'coon song', as finally translated into Caucasian, was
virtually shouted "with an impudent determination to keep out of
time and out of key." Unlike the latter day "Jazz baby," the popular
"coon shouter" was a lusty, well-rounded lady. Besides her curves,
Miss Irwin boasted a voice that "descended on you like a wild, raucous yell."

[23]

RAGTIME was most authentic American strain in popular music at the turn of the century. Above are three hit tunes, early, middle and late, to mark its passing. Monstrously exciting to the senses, the hilarity of these songs was a good anecdote for After-The-Ball bathos, did much to lighten the balladry of the era. On the stage, the monochled European type of operetta was running towards rip-tide. Yet American tunesmiths were hunting for something of their own. They seemed to find it in the indigenous rhythms of the former slaves. Translated to Broadway as ragtime, it set the country afire. Young ladies who practiced Mozart for their piano teacher, worked overtime on coon songs for their own amusement. People flocked to vaudeville to see whites in black-face, or real black and tan teams like Williams and Walker and Cole and Johnson, perform this forerunner of the jazz age. An attempt was made to 'rag' everything, including Rock of Ages and The Star Spangled Banner. But it took a real piano virtuoso to 'rag' effectively, and even then a certain basic rhythm was essential. Anyone wishing can try his hand on the songs shown above, or seize upon the Cole and Johnson number, which runs

If you lak-a me,—like I lak-a you . . . . And If you Love-e Me . . . .
One live as two,—two live as one . . . . Under the Banyan Tree.

[24]

IN SINGING RAGTIME, there often developed the use of an interpolated vowel. An instinctive negro response to the rhythm, the practice is indicated in this song.

HELLO MA BABY

Here is how the chorus goes

He-ge-dello, ma baby
He-ge-dello, ma honey
He-ge-dello, ma ragtime gal
Se-ge-dend me a kess by wire
He-ge-doney, ma heart's on fire!

SONGS AND STARS who made them. Scant are the memories of
these tunes, except in connection with the stars who put them across.
The *fin de siecle* found the popular music business organized into a well
defined pattern, with publishing duties split up for division of labor.
Composers and lyricists whose work had found favor were hired as
staff writers and arrangers. They ground out the great bulk of songs,
often helped instruct the performers who were to make the songs
popular throughout the stage and vaudeville circuit. But the chief
agent of ballyhoo was the man who made contact between the song
and the singer. In order to get big-time artists to push a particular
title, they were often put on the payroll of the company. Sometimes
the job was done even more handsomely, such as presenting the star
a diamond ring or a race horse. Above three songs needed help!
BILLY BURKE is justly more famous as an actress than for her songs
The wife of Flo Ziegfeld, she has continued to play in movies and
radio. MARIE DRESSLER, also remembered for her movie work,
was once on the stage; *Heaven Will Protect The Working Girl* is her best
known number. MARIE CAHILL was probably better known than
either of these in the early 1900's. She was among the first to take
such compositions as *Under the Banyan Tree* from colored composers,
put them over on the musical comedy stage.   [26]

WITH POPULARIZATION of a song a veritable 200 to 1 shot, it paid to get the best performers possible to back it up. Many songs had to find just the right personality before they could be 'put over.' *Has Anybody Here Seen Kelly* is a case in point. It was first tried out in America with Emma Carus and proved a dismal flop. Later is was made over slightly for NORA BAYES, who sang it to instantaneous success. The song, *In The Good Old Summer Time*, though written and used by a well known minstrel end man, required a rendition by BLANCH RING to make it a huge success. Use of this cover gives the impression of Miss Ring as a singer of light ballads only. This she was not. As the reigning musical comedy favorite, she is perhaps better remembered singing "Got Rings on my Fingers and bells on my toes, Yip-i-Addy-i-ay." As for the song *Some Of These Days*, it was again a case of waiting for the right personality. Not until SOPHIE TUCKER, "last of the red-hot mammas," made this song her own, did it catch on. Conspicuous by her absence in the above galaxy is EVA TANGUAY, the Betty Hutton of the two-a-day. A person with tremendous energy—and no voice—Eva used to flounce around the stage, shouting her song "I DON'T CARE," she would yell, "Though my voice may be funny, it gets me the money! so I–Don't Care." The public ate it up.

SOME of Victor Herbert's songs have been called "too good" for his operetta's. A case in point is the score of *Mille Modeste*.

Few today can recall the hit tune of this production, *Mascot Of The Regiment*. But buried in the same dated piece was a song originally entitled *If I Were On The Stage*. Removed from its context and retitled *Kiss Me Again*, the song has risen to timelessness, is played and sung around the world.

VICTOR HERBERT, most American of composers who wrote musi-
cals in emulation of Johann Straus, was a big name in the 1900's.
Here are song covers from three of his finest productions. *Mille Modeste*,
Babes in Toyland and *Red Mill* are best known scores of the period.
All carried songs of lasting appeal.

Herbert operetta's were as much a part of American life as the
speculative mania of Wall Street which led to the inevitable panic of
1907. Proper ladies wore high collars held up by whalebones, left
business to men. Fritzi Scheff stood on her drum and sang herself into
stardom as *Mascot of the Regiment* in MILLE MODESTE.

TYPICAL of the European influence in American musical comedy at
the turn of the century, was *Prince of Pilzen*. The plot centered around
an experienced Widow and a gay bunch of love-sick young bucks.
Best known of the foreign imports of monacled operetta was *The
Merry Widow* by Lehar. But Herbert was no copyest of alien scores.
Superbly gifted and far better trained than most popular song-writers
of his day, his record is studded with brilliant orchestral arrangements,
unforgettable melodies and fascinating waltz rhythms. A convivial
soul with heart of gold, music and friendship came first with Victor
Herbert, money secondarily.

[29]

TITLE INSPIRED by famous minstrel endman, George "Honey Boy" Evans, still played as "taps" over his grave in Streator, Ill. A 1907 hit, by vaudeville's Jack Norworth and Albert Von Tilzer.

A LEMON IN THE GARDEN OF LOVE

COMEDY ELEMENT, circa 1906. Richard Carle thus found means to parody the sentimental ballad, holdover from 19th century. The Casper Milquetoast of his day, he wrote song for show *Spring Chicken*.

THREE COHAN SONGS that did much to set pattern for future American musical shows. At the beginning of the century, the Vienese type of frothy operetta had most of the producers bewitched and the public bewildered. As a counterblast to such imports, George M· Cohan began writing shows with an American theme. Best remembered are FORTY-FIVE MINUTES FROM BROADWAY and LITTLE JOHNNY JONES. The first drew a vigorous protest from the locale of the play New Rochelle; "they have whiskers like hay, and imagine Broadway only forty-five minutes from here." LITTLE JOHNNY JONES was a topical show, built around the homesickness of a famous jockey, Tod Sloan, who had gone to England to race horses for dukes and kings. Nostalgia for America was pushed to a new high with Cohan in the steller role singing "I'm a Yankee Doodle Dandy, Yankee Doodle Do or Die; real live nephew of my Uncle Sam, born on the Fourth of July." Critics lambasted the author-star for his flag-waving, but the public ate it up. Cohan had given current musical comedy the shot of Yankee pep it badly needed. Ragtime marriage ceremonies and court trials were a refreshing sight for an audience surfeited with the MERRY WIDOW and her monacled lovers. They even approved the affectionate *You're a Grand Old Rag*, but this was shortly changed to *flag* for dignity's sake.

[32]

GEORGE M. COHAN never got over his blatent Americanism, his bragging that "when you're away from Broadway you're only camping out," and just when his younger contemporaries were ready to write him off, overnight he wrote *Over There*—hit tune of World War I.

SONGS AS UNPRETENTIOUS as a wild rose! That was way
Carrie Jacobs Bond originally billed the above numbers. Far from unpretentious, however, is the record they have piled up through ensuing
years. One of the few lady composers of Tin Pan Alley, and a real
lady at that, Mrs. Bond at first found no publisher interested in her
songs, went out to popularize them by giving concerts throughout the
hinterland. By publishing songs herself, she preserved a rich asset for
her family. Such numbers as *Just A Wearying For You* soon claimed
tremendous royalties, and *I Love You Truly* became a must for every
wedding ceremony. These songs continue to hold top AA rating in
ASCAP, the association which licenses public performance of songs.
Under the rating system used to apportion income from such rights,
it is estimated that Carrie Jacobs Bond's estate takes in as much as
that prolific all-time favorite, Irving Berlin.

Mrs. Bond was one of the few composers of Tin Pan Alley ever to
be invited to give concerts at the White House. She was a guest of
Teddy Roosevelt, later of Calvin Coolidge, and singing—of course—
"When you come to the end of a perfect day

And you sit alone with your thought
While the chimes ring out with a carol gay

For the joy that the day has brought."

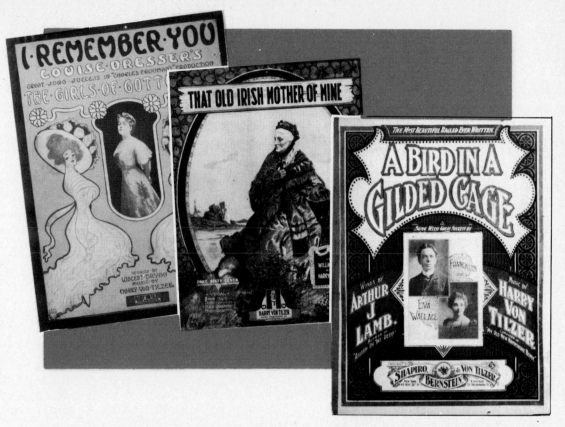

TOP SONG WRITER of close harmony era was Harry Von Tilzer. Terribly prolific, he was one of first song-writers to have his own publishing house, is credited with naming Tin Pan Alley. Lyricists vied with each other to bring him their best verses, knowing that if he took to their spirit he could write a tune to set them in solid gold. Von Tilzer had over a dozen million copy hits, including *Wait Till The Sun Shines Nellie*, *On A Sunday Afternoon*, *Just Around the Corner*, and *Down Where the Wurzburger Flows*. His *Alexander*, preceding *Alexander's Ragtime Band*, was a top 'coon' number. He wrote the first 'telephone' song. His *Old Irish Mother of Mine* is still a stock number for all tenors. But if one song has to be singled out for Von Tilzer, it is *Bird In A Gilded Cage*. The phrase, in fact, has come to stand for this era of song. *Bird* is supposed to have been composed during a party which ended in a Chicago roadhouse. While other members of the party engaged in ribaldry, Von Tilzer sat down at the piano, set a sheet of verses on the music rack, and began to play and sing a tune that had even the fancy ladies in tears. Song told story of an old man's darling, refrain always ending:

"And her beauty was sold for an old man's gold—
Just a bird in a gilded cage."

THE 20TH CENTURY'S first decade of song ended on a new and faster note than that of its beginning. Where sentimental ballads and their parodies had once been popular, interest had now shifted to waltz songs and ragtime melodies. True, both of these song-types were known by 1900. Ragtime was then coming out of the Deep South, operetta waltz songs from Europe. But these two currents had to cross in Gotham before making their lively impact generally felt. It took time to popularize the new mode, overcome the preference for close harmony, set up song writing as big business and name it Tin Pan Alley.

An analysis of the songs recalled on the preceding pages shows a general song development in the direction of speedup. Acceleration occurred in all three aspects of song, talk, time and tune. By the decade's end, the new currents of energy had raised its temperature and quickened its pulse. Some of the older composers, like Harris and Dresser, could not escape the groves of sentimental balladry; younger tunesmiths like George M. Cohan and the Von Tilzer's showed a surprising versatility in swinging with the tide of fancy. On the whole, the speed shift acted to improve popular song. Nonsease syllables (always a lyricists stock-in-trade) moved from the banal "tra-la-la" to such inescapable concoctions as "vo-de-o-do;" tempo began to play a role of increasing importance in the creation of 'mood' effects; the melody developed fluidity of movement. All this called for some change in the habits of amateur performance. No longer was unaccompanied solo or part singing sufficient to convey a song's message effectively. Something had to be added, some generally available, mass-produced instrument that would help turn our songs—like everything else—from the hand-made towards the machine-made.

1910

Piano Accompaniment...

THE GIBSON GIRL entertained the ARROW COLLAR man at the piano, and a good time was had by all. It was the second decade of our century and polite usage dictated that the parlor be turned over to the young lady and her beau. Seated at the keyboard, not only might she display the cultural accomplishments that made her a desirable prize; the skill acquired was held so tenuously that her full attention was needed to read the notes. Little time was left for spooning, and the old folks in the next room received advance warning of it whenever the music stopped. A sheet of music was considered a very proper gift from a gentleman caller. It gave the young folks something to do; and who knew but what such sublimated expressions of love might not lead to a bonified proposal of marriage. To this picture writers of popular songs contributed without stint. New tunes were published in great numbers, MORE THAN enough to keep the music rack overflowing. It was the era of PIANO ACCOMPANIMENT.

The basis for the popularity of the piano in this decade lay partly in its prevalence. Desire to accompany the voice by some musical instrument is ageless and universal. But primitive drums, the harp or banjo lacked the piano's versatility in forming a proper background for the new songs. Besides, just as the need was greatest, mass production methods brought upright pianos to a price within the means of the average American family. A piano in the parlor and lessons for daughters were a must in any home that aspired to refinement. Piano scores were kept as simple as possible and everyone was encouraged to accompany himself in song. This was when the home was the center of entertainment and mechanical purveyors of music were still in their infancy. Some very beautiful and enduring songs were written during this decade, as shown by the pictorial reminders that follow. The vast majority held to simple melodic structures well within the range of the average voice and piano technique. Ragtime Still found new converts; but a far more popular vehicle was a piano number arranged for "Mixed Quartet." *By the light of the silvery moon . . ., we two could spoon . . .' Da-de-da, da, da "June . . . how soon."*

MUSIC FOR THE FLICKERS. So popular was sheet music in this decade that movie makers had songs composed on their productions. Practically none of the covers shown above denote songs that can be remembered. One, *The Perils of Pauline*, was an out-right take-off of the extravagant escapes staged in the Pearl White serials, and hence of no great use to the movie makers. A few of these songs were played in the movie house during the showing of the film. Far more typical of the period of silent "flickers" was the playing of "mood" music. The pianist sat at the side of the screen with one eye on the reflected beam of light; the other on a book of scores; items labelled "galloping horses," "lover lost," and "sweet reunion," were chosen accordingly.

[40]

SONG of a famous movie and its star, Miss Mabel Normand;
"Mickey, pretty Mickey, with your hair of raven hue, Mickey, pretty
Mickey, how could anyone help but falling in love with you."

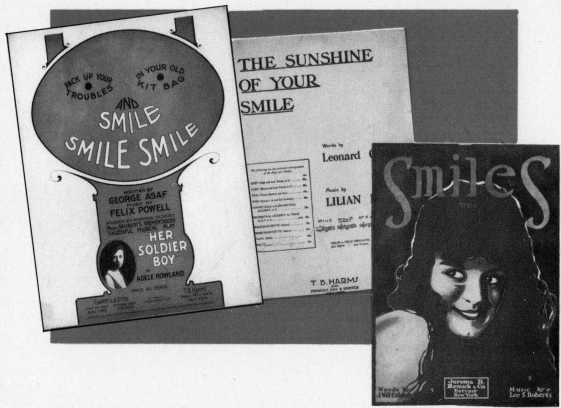

SMILES SONGS have been popular in every era, probably because few people are really very happy and often sing to keep up their spirits. The 1910 period boasts three of the most famous smiles songs ever published, as shown above. Everyone can hum "There are smiles that make us happy, there are smiles that make us blue." Still a great favorite at community sings is "What's the use of worrying, it never was worthwhile, so pack up your troubles in your old kit bag and smile, smile, smile." More tuneful, but also more difficult to sing is "Give me your smile, the lovelight in your eyes . . . . . my world forever, the sunshine of your smile."

Many interesting stories have arisen as to how such smiles songs first came to be written; one of the most authentic concerns *Powder Your Face With Sunshine*, written by a hospitalized veteran of World War II.

BOW TO THE FORGOTTEN MAN. In song writing, it's the composer of the music that gets the credit and popular acclaim of a hit tune. Yet the regulars of Tin Pan Alley know that the words are often more important than the tune in putting a song across. Consider a recent example of this: *If I Knew You Were Coming I'd Have Baked A Cake* (1950). There is just no tune at all to this "song", yet its catchy phrase put it at the top of the hit parade in less than a month.

[42]

ABOVE are covers from songs that owe their continued popularity as much to the words as to the tune. The original song *Melancholy* is now known as "Come to me my melancholy baby, cuddle up and don't feel blue." And who can forget "But there's one rose that dies not in *Picardy* . . . . . . 'tis the rose that I keep in my heart." *Keep the Home Fires Burning* was originally written for the Yale Glee Club, got to England and the trenches of World War I because its author went as a Rhodes Scholar to Oxford. One of the greatest lyricists of this era was Joseph McCarty, here represented by "My sweet little *Alice Blue Gown*, when I first wandered down into town." Some other McCarty standbys: *I'm Always Chasing Rainbows; Ireland Must Be Heaven.*

[43]

TRANSPORTATION SONGS were extremely popular with early 19th Century audiences. To a public whose mode of travel was undergoing such rapid changes, it is no wonder that the automobile, the airplane, even the trolley car should hold widespread interest. What is significant is the extent to which popular song writers made use of the subject. As all who are familiar with Tin Pan Alley know, any event of national significance always gets described in song. Often the connection between the item and the lyrics is extremely tenuous; sometimes it is found in the title alone. Such topical songs seldom last, soon pass into the land of Forgotten Lore. Above are five song covers that will, for some, bring back pleasant memories of the past.

THE LATEST THING, circa 1910: That women could be induced
to ride in airplanes was a matter of wishful thinking. With the automobile still a novelty, personal conquest of the air was just a song.

DUETS were very popular in piano-playing days. Here are three numbers well within the range of average talent, that continue to live:

Whispering Hope, "Soft falls the voice of an angel, breathing a message of hope"

Lullaby Land, "Those golden days of childhood, Somehow I cannot forget."

My Isle of Golden Dreams, "Somehow I know, someday I'll go, back o'er the sea."

Most duets of the period were set for feminine voices, soprano and alto. Like the most popular of popular music, they stuck pretty closely to the octave range, seldom featured a difficult melodic jump. Male and female duets were occasionally performed at home-talent shows, but such public harmonizing was not thought proper for the unmarried, or even for the engaged. Instead, a pair of young ladies would harmonize a song to the accompaniment of Delsarte, a system which taught the graceful gestures to accompany every emotion. Young men were supposed to sit back and marvel at their combined purity of tone and motion.

SHEET MUSIC SALES during this decade reached an all-time high and sheet music prices reached an all-time low. Every five and dime store had its music counter complete with piano rattling salesgirl. Prices went down from 50 cents to 15 cents a copy. Above are a host of songs, good, bad, indifferent, as displayed in a music sales counter.

WHEN NEW YORK WAS A SUMMER RESORT. People from the hinterlands used to flock to the city for a summer vacation. Atop the great hotels and other high buildings, roof gardens were built wherein people could look down on the city lights. These were the night clubs of the era, where one could dine and dance, or simply watch a daring "girlie" floor show. Many an "intimate revue" and song-and-dance musical got its start in a roof garden, went on to become an annual affair, like Ziegfeld's Follies, in a theatre all its own. Above are song covers from three of the yearly editions of the Follies, all but forgotten today. The descent of musical revues from the roof to the street was accompanied by some increase in the tunefulness of songs. Who, however, pretends to remember any Follies song as such. That was probably never intended. Take just one case in point. Who can yet hum the tune for this one?

Starlight, starlight,   Gleam on, stream on,
wonderful and silvery far light   O'er the world and let us dream on.

No, the thing one remembers about Ziegfeld's extravaganzas is not the tunes, but their proudly plumed beauties stalking around the stage looking decorative but dumb.

RAYMOND HUBBELL was one of the most prolific writers of
musical shows in his day. But though he is credited with 30 successful
scores, only the song above, once considered unpromising, has lived.

[49]

BIRTH OF THE BLUES. Song covers on this page typify the pre-jazz era. Its high priest was W. C. Handy, whose catchy song, *The Memphis Blues*, was first played by colored musicians to help Boss Crump elect his mayoralty candidate back in Memphis in 1909. Many think that progenitors of "the blues" were Negro spirituals, and one suggested derivation of the word "Jazz" is from their "Jubbing" or jubilee singing. Correctly, however, a blues is a one-man song, and a way to express a grievance rather than a joy. "Oh, de Mississippi is so deep and wide; Oh, de Mississippi is so dee-and Lawdy; Now my gal lives on de odder side." In this typical three line verse lies the origin of the twelve-bar blues melody; its "oh, Lawdy" provides a basis for the "jazz break"; its flatted seventh ending gives the "blues note." W. C. Handy created none of these innovations; but he did set them into a musical score, thereby enabling composers unfamiliar with Negro folk song to experiment with the essential elements of jazz. Neither Handy's blues nor Muir's equally adroit pre-jazz song, *Waiting For The Robert E. Lee*, were to attain widespread acceptance until another decade. They were too raw, peppy and difficult for the polite parlor pianist either to enjoy or to perform. Publishers were wary, so Handy put out his own music; Muir's opus was taken by Mills because of the latter's earlier success with *Georgia Camp Meeting*.

[50]

EARLY CONVERT to negro jazz-blues was Vincent Lopez, here shown against the piece he popularized. First discovered playing in a Broadway restaurant, he did much to take rawness out of oncoming jazz.

[51]

TRANSITION TO DANCE

Up to 1910 dancing was an occasional and questionable delight. The waltz, only dance permitting intimate physical contact, was played so fast you felt you were on a scenic railway rather than in the tunnel of love. Then came the Turkey trot, nothing more than a walk in a close embrace. There were all sorts of varients, the Grizzly Bear, Gotham Gobble, Gaby Glide and the Bunny Hug (as sung as a bug bug in a rug . . . stop, stop . . . that bunny-bunny hug). Sousa's marches were pressed into service as One and Two-step, even as Fox-trots. When the Tango was barred from Yale's prom in 1914, it was front page news. And now there developed a new type of institution, the Afternoon Tea Dance. Restaurants began to feature dancing between courses and between meals, even to provide partners for unescorted ladies and gentlemen. Wives visited these places with gigilos while their husbands supposedly worked, and husbands sneaked out of their offices where they would dance with hostesses, "Wiggling about as much like a slippery-slush as one can."

The menu card from staid Rector's restaurant tells quite a story. The wiggly wigglers were not interested in food, with a corresponding deterioration in the menu. The Chef d'orchestra, not the Chef de Cusine, was the man of the hour.

[52]

Cheif credit for changing the dance tastes of the nation goes to Irene and Vernon Castle, a young team of ballroom dancers. To watch them was to want to dance! More accurately, to want to dance with Mrs. Castle. Irene was the most original beauty of her time, the first to bob her hair, the first really slender model of feminine pulchritude, the first to set styles in dress as well as in dancing. Vernon was the perfect foil for this display. To the public they stood for everything smart and sophisticated. Lionized by society and by fan club, they became a national institution.

The Castles and their followers required that new tunes be as danceable as they were singable. Some of the popular music of the decade filled the requirement, much did not. For the full fruits of Castle pioneering, one must see phonograph in fox-trot mania of 1920's.

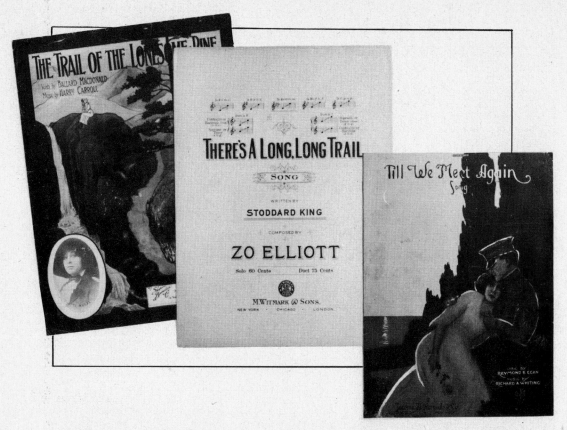

THREE GREAT SONGS that everybody sang. They still brag in Tin Pan Alley of the phenomenal sales records these songs set. Somewhat curiously, they are not heard today nearly as often as less famous contemporaries. Only at a community song-fest are you likely to encounter "In the Blue Ridge Mountains of Virginia, on the trail of the lonesome pine", "There's a long, long trail awinding into the land of my dreams", and "So wait and pray each night for me, till we meet again". It is significant that these great songs (and many another like them) never belonged to a single performer, as in the days of early song plugging. Songs of this era were much more widely dispersed and were seldom given to any one star to popularize. Instead the music publishers had begun to rely somewhat on mechanical recordings, plus an all-out drive to sell songs over the counter in department and variety stores. Every "5 and 10" of the period had its sheet music section, complete with tinny piano and a local performer who played and sang snatches of whatever was most in demand. Artists like Gene Buck did their best to make eye-appealing covers. Irving Berlin's *Snookey-Ookums* and Jerome Kern's *They Didn't Believe Me* far outsold better songs they wrote in later decades, when the sheet music industry had started its decline.

[54]

I WANT A GIRL

(JUST LIKE THE GIRL THAT MARRIED DEAR OLD DAD)

WORDS BY
WILL DILLON
MUSIC BY
HARRY VON TILZER

VOTED one of the most popular songs of all time. It's the sentiment of the words that endears this number, makes it a favorite with Rotary Clubs and other group "sings". Lyricist Dillon had many another hit.

ERNEST R. BALL carried an earlier tradition of light ballad into this decade, produced a number of all-time favorites. He first wrote the tune for Jimmy Walker's *Will You Love Me In December As You Do In May*, went on to such hits as *Till The Sands Of The Desert Grow Cold*, *Let The Rest Of The World Go By* and *Dear Little Boy Of Mine*. He struck an all-time high in writing for the Chauncey Olcott musicals such songs as *Mother Macree*. A peculiar tear-jerking quality in all Ball songs has endeared him with every Irish tenor, John McCormick not excepted. Far more typically period, however, was *All The World Will Be Jealous Of Me*, great for lovesick crooning about the piano.

[56]

DEPLORABLE TASTE. The New York Dramatic Mirror for March 19th, 1913 devoted its main story to the "lewdness and bad taste" displayed in songs like the above. Comparing the mood and spirit of such old favorites as *Juanita* with "when I get you alone tonight" songs from the "new-type musical shows," it was freely predicted that the world was on its way to the dogs. The article particularly deplored this little number:
"Every day I go for a lark in the park–and Johnny goes too, Johnny...
  Every night I come home to my bed–and Johnny comes too, Johnny..."
This was reputedly sung by a "jauntily bejeweled young woman in a close fitting 'hobble' that overemphasized the revealing function of her clothes, an expression of cynical frankness on her sensuous face." Another tune that came in for censure was "Everybody's doing it . . . . . doing what . . . . . Turkey Trot," performed in the first act finale of the 1913 Follies "with nurse-maids, policemen, piano movers and even cab horses cavorting about the stage in a most indecent manner." The article went on to point out that if songs were not "suggestive", they were at the other extreme of "inanity". It has taken short time for these songs to pass out of memory, as compared to more enduring ones recorded in this book.

[57]

FAMOUS STARS who plugged songs in the 1910 era include Nora Bayes and her husband, Jack Northworth, Will Dillon, Whiting and Burt, Elsie Janis and The Duncan Sisters. The Bayes-Northworth combine received top billing everywhere. Will Dillon, youngest of the famed Dillon brothers, is as noted for his *Little Girl* as for his vaudeville performances. Whiting and Burt were a Winter Garden duo with a great following, while the Duncan Sisters were the darlings of the Keith-Orpheum curcuit. Greatest personality of the decade, by many counts, was Elsie Janis. A famed impersonator and songstress, she gave unstintingly of her time to overseas work during World War I. Afterwards in Hollywood she wrote *Love, Your Magic Spell is Everywhere*.

[58]

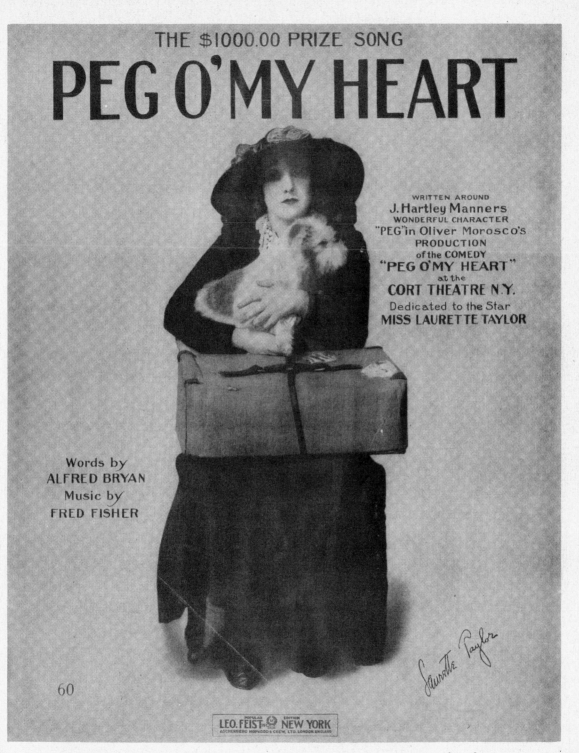

SONG of the period did get associated with the name of a famous stage personality. Laurette Taylor and *Peg O' My Heart* are inextricably linked in memory.

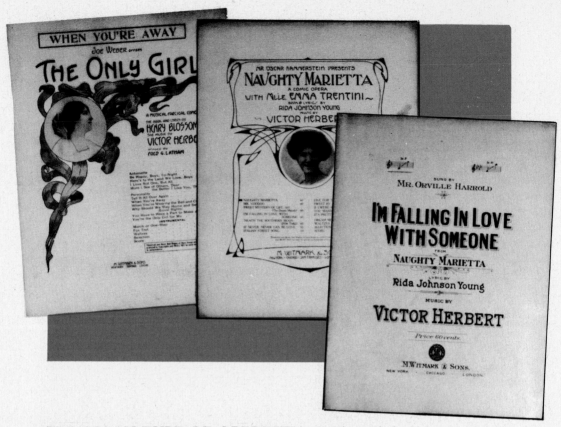

EUROPEAN TYPE OF OPERETTA dominated American musical comedy in the early 20th century, reached its high point of favor and excellence under the master hand of Victor Herbert. Coming to this country in 1886 to conduct bands and orchestras, by 1903 his fame as a composer was such that he devoted the rest of his life to this calling. Above are covers from world-famous Herbert scores. Everyone knows "When you're away, dear, how weary the lonesome hours," from *The Only Girl*, and the stellar number-first sung by Mille. Emma Trentini, "*Naughty Marietta*, Come be good-say she, mais non, say me." The real thrill of light opera was to pay fifty cents and get in the gallery to hear great stars like Trentini singing songs you could understand and hum yourself. Herbert music has sometimes been called "second rate Strauss" or "derived from Gounod." Be that as it may, he left his mark on American musical history; also upon its organizational aspects. In 1914, Victor Herbert founded ASCAP (American Society of Composers, Authors and Publishers) which fought the unlicensed use of popular songs by phonograph companies, radio and other mechanicals. ASCAP eventually became the powerful central clearing house for collection and disbursement of royalties from all such performances.

[60]

VICTOR HERBERT'S MASTERPIECE
AH! SWEET MYSTERY of LIFE

Lyric
by
Rida
Johnson
Young

The Dream
Melody
from
Naughty
Marietta

SOLO 4 Keys, A♭(eb toeb) B♭(f to f) C (g to g) D (a to a) 50¢ T. Each.
DUET 2 Keys, B♭ Melody Low. D Melody High. 65¢ T. Each.
OCTAVO, Two Part. 12¢. Three Part 15¢. Four Part Male
Female, and Mixed Voices 15¢ Each Net.

THE WITMARK
BLACK
AND
WHITE
SERIES

ENSEMBLE. Violin and Piano 50¢ T. Cello and Piano 50¢ T.
Violin, Cello and Piano 65¢ T.
INSTRUMENTAL. The Dream Melody (Intermezzo) 50¢ T. Waltz, 50¢ T.
VOCAL and DANCE ORCHESTRA (Waltz) 50¢ Each Net. BAND 60¢ Net.

A GREAT THEME. "Ah sweet mystery of life, at last I found thee.....
Ah, at last I know the secret of it all"...... melody and words build
to the great sentimental climax, "For it is love alone that rules for aye."

[61]

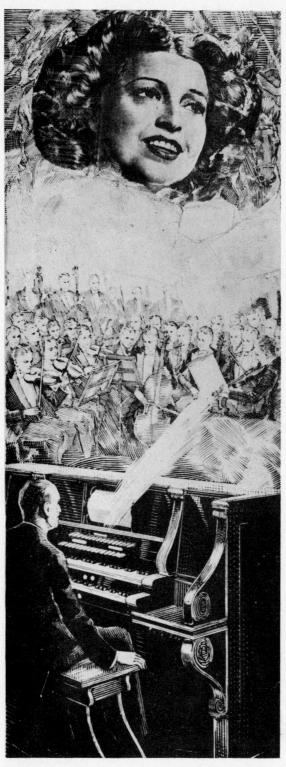

"A PRETTY GIRL—
IS LIKE A MEL-O-DY
THAT HAUNTS—
YOU NIGHT AND DAY"

MANY PEOPLE heard or sung their first rendition of this Irving Berlin classic with some such instrument as the one pic-such instrument as the one pictured at the left. This era marks the beginnings of an advance of "mechanicals" over the self-performance of popular music. In the first decade of the century, makers of the primitive phonographs and player pianos did recordings of any tune they wished, without even a by-your-leave to the copyright holders. All this was changed after 1914, the date of the founding of ASC-AP. Mechanical recorders were now perfected, and engaged the skill of some of the first talent of the day. First to gain—and first to loose—in popular acceptance were the player organs and player pianos. The Q.R.S. Co. was the greatest maker of such recordings. Some of their rolls are already collectors items . . . and who now owns a player to play them?

MEMORY SONGS that never die. From Sigmund Romberg's operetta *Maytime*, comes the immortal "Sweetheart, Sweetheart, Sweetheart,—will you remember the day,—when we were happy in May–my–dear–est–one." From a fraternity song comes "the girl of my dreams is the sweetest girl of all the girls I know. . . . And the moonlight beams on the girl of my dreams, she's the *Sweetheart of Sigma Chi*." "Most people can also hum the great DeSilva-Conrad hit, "I am with you, wandering through *Memory Lane*," or "*Beautiful Ohio*, till we meet again." But the all inclusive number everybody loves is "*Memories*, dreams of long ago....still you're my own, in my garden of Memories."

Yip Yip Yaphank

Reprinted from [...]
August 23, 1918

LEXINGTON THEATRE

Phone Plaza 5020

[...]reet and Lexington Avenue

IDY

[...]ing Monday Evening, September 2, 1918

NEW YORK, August 23.—"I have heard that Berlin is among the foremost songwriters of the world, and now I believe it," said Major General J. Franklin Bell, speaking from a stage box at the Century Theatre, N. Y., Monday evening following the finale of "Yip Yip Yaphank," everything by Irving Berlin, having its premier that night. Just previously General Bell addressed the audience from the stage, expressing his appreciation of the reception given his soldier boys. The General appeared pleased. He said the proceeds were for a community house at Camp Upton, where the camp could act as host to the families and friends of the officers and soldiers.

To seasoned army men like General Bell, to whom theatricals are merely a diversion at best, "Yip Yip Yaphank," played by khaki clad boys, must have been a revelation. It was that anyway to the overseasoned Broadwayites who attended the initial performance. Here were 350 men, all from Camp Upton, giving a show that moved with the precision of a clock. In the opening scene, a minstrel first part, 277 were on the stage at the finale—and not a miss!

That first part woke up the house. Their early attitude of forebearance because "It's for the Service" gave way to pleasure, then admiration, and as the show progressed the house realized it was watching one of the best and most novel entertainments Broadway has ever witnessed.

—SIME

Reprinted from
The New York Times
July 27, 1918

NEW YORK, July 27.—About 150 men of the National Army in training at Camp Upton will take part in a musical revue by Irving Berlin given ing the week of August 19. The title of the production is "Yip Yip Yap-hank" and the profits will be used for the erection of a community home where the friends and relatives of men in training can be made comfortable when visiting at the camp. Irving Berlin, who was drafted several months ago, and was recently promoted to the rank of Sergeant, is the author of the show which will appear in two acts and ten scenes. Berlin will [...] professional people. "Yip Yip" [...] entirely military in nature, and [...] with life at Upton.

LUCAS JACOBS

ENTIRE COMPANY
ENTIRE COMPANY

PVTS. BRENNAN, BRENNA, PHILLIPS, SNYDER, SCHOR AND WARD

"What a Difference a Uniform [...] PRIVATE [...]
"Mandy"

Program Continued

The Captain's Address to the Company

Tambourine Drill
Opening Chorus. "Hello, Hello, Hello"
Solos

CLINE
CRONIN
HAGGERTY
McCARTHY
CHURCHILL
CAHILL
CONDNEN
DERMODY
DEGNAN
DEICK
DAVISON
DAVISON
DONALDSON
ELLIS
EPSTEIN
EWELL
FRANCOIS
FREDERICH
FEILBERMAN
FITZPATRICK
FROST
GOLNEY
GOLNEY
GAULEN
GROSSMAN
GARBLICK
GINSBERG

[...]IST
BALLING
BARNETT
BARSALOON
B. BROWN
BRAGG
D. BROWN
A. BROWN
BOYLE
BOLLES
BUCKLEY
BURNS
BORGRAFF
BURNETT
BRYDE
BREYER
CAMPBELL
COLLINS
CULLMAN
CONDEN
CONWAY

THERE WAS A WAR ON in this decade: World War I, to be exact. Of the many good marching songs written, those on the opposite page will be longest remembered. Above is a memento from Sgt. Irving Berlin's all soldier show staged at Camp Upton and New York.

IF YOU measure greatness in terms of universality of appeal and the persistence of memory, the 1910 decade constituted a period of great popular songs. Herein were produced such all-time favorites as *There's a Long, Long Trail a Winding*, frequently cited as the top tune of all time, *Till We Meet Again*, which had as large a sheet music sale as any song ever published, and that perennial favorite *Peg of My Heart*. The greatest war songs ever written (*Over There*, *Tipperary*, *Keep the Home Fires Burning*) came in this period. Victor Herbert and Sigmund Romberg wrote their most tuneful operettas in those years. That stalwart of the Old school, Harry Von Tilzer, wrote *Apple Blossom Time and I Want a Girl*. Modernists Jerome Kern, Cole Porter and George Gershwin got their start here. Standing in between the old and the new school of popular song was Irving Berlin, with something for every mood. His songs were still simple enough to be sung by the *hoi polloi*, yet had received considerable new sublety at the hands of his arrangers.

Like Berlin's, the vast majority of 1910 songs still carried simple melodic structures, well within the range of the average voice and scored for a very ordinary piano player. A few piano virtuosos, such as Vincent Lopez, were using the instrument, of course, to make people want to dance as well as to sing popular songs. Not until this decade, we may recall, was social dancing divested of its association with sin, or did respectable young people partake much of its joys. The war, of course, provided occasion for release of inhibitions. But some credit must go to the piano-led orchestra and its infectious invitation to dance. Popular music was becoming less simplified, more musicianlike. The stage was being set for acceptance of even greater complexities.

1920

Phonograph Fever . . .

THE DECADE following the first world War marked a period of unprecedented expansion in American enterprise. Prosperity brought with it a lessening of inhibitions and social restraints. Flaming youth took to the cigarette and the hip flask. And more than either of these, it took to dance music. Earlier ragtime melodies and blues songs had set the stage for the fox-trot mania. But equal importance goes to the perfecting and mass-production of mechanical means of playing the hot new tunes. Victrolas came down to a price practically everyone could afford. Records cost 25 cents. A portable was all that was needed to turn any place into a dance hall. When the dancers had worn out their welcome, the records could be packed and moved on to the next place. It was the age of jazz, the era of PHONOGRAPH FEVER.

The development of mechanical purveyors of song, which had started early in the century, now bid fair to engulf the entire music industry. From tiny beginnings and tiny renditions of song, the phonograph had become a household necessity which gave faithful reproductions of the best music by the best bands. No longer was it necessary to go to an expensive stage show or restaurant to hear the top performers of the day. You could buy a recording at the Five and Ten, take it home and play it whenever the spirit moved. Record sales rose to outlandish heights; music publishers began to collect more from royalties thereon than from song sheet sales. As the general public shifted from making its own music to listening to recorded versions, it was no longer important to write tunes so simply. Composers were tempted to use octave jumps and harmonic arrangements suited only to professional performers. And thus it came about that the top tunes of the period were no longer simple melodies to be sung by all the people, but clever complicated pieces to challenge real musicianship. This was the age when Gershwin and Paul Whiteman were both encouraged to try their boldest wings. By the curious flip of Fate, widespread acceptance of mechanical reproduction of music actually invited popular song to become much more difficult at the very time when well trained musicians were moving into Tin Pan Alley.

[69]

AUTHORITIES DISAGREE as to where the word "jazz" came from, but all are as one regarding its appeal. Beginning in Africa as tight rhythm and ending in America as abandoned counterpoint, its ompha, omp-phh beat goes straight to the senses. Jazz made the saxophone, the trombone and the trumpet instruments of great virtuosity. The bands which first played the music indicated above ranged all the way from racket to rhapsody. Ted Lewis' band was a crude nuisance with its main emphasis on noise. Less raucous aggregations of instruments led to the blandness of Lopez and the insinuations of Paul Whiteman. The trombone learned to laugh and coo as well as to blare.

THE PIANO had by no means outlived its usefulness as a purveyor of popular tunes. It had graduated from the parlor to the dance hall and concert stage. Here are three jazz numbers frequently introduced.

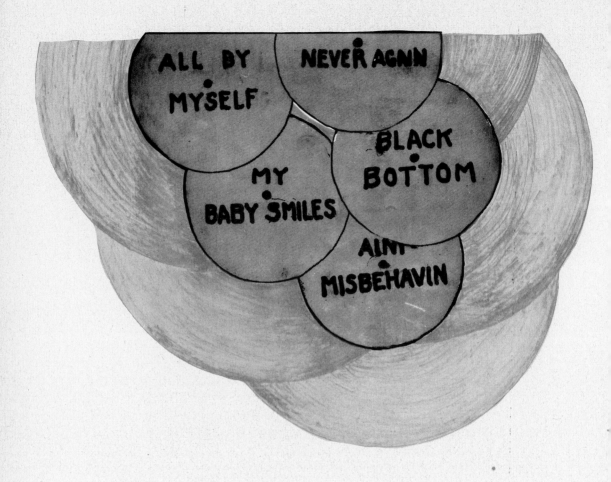

THOUGH THERE WERE phonographs and other "mechanical" purveyors of music before 1920, not until this decade did such gadgets cut seriously into sheet music sales. The onslaught almost became a slaughter. As music came to be written for the feet rather than for the ear, more and more people preferred to dance—even at home—to a mechanical tune rather than one played from piano music. Record prices went down and sales rose spectacularly. In slightly more than a year of sales, Irving Berlin's *All By Myself* sold under a million copies of sheet music but a million and a half "mechanicals." The record sales of *At Sundown* approached the 2,000,000 mark in no time. Tin Pan Alley had to adjust itself to changing times. Now, more important than a stage personality, was the coaxing of a famed dance band to "cut a platter." As there were not enough famed bands to go around, some song publishers conducted a still hunt of discovery. Paul White-man was discovered in an Atlantic City Hotel. Vincent Lopez in a Broadway restaurant. Negro bands were created to record the new "blues."

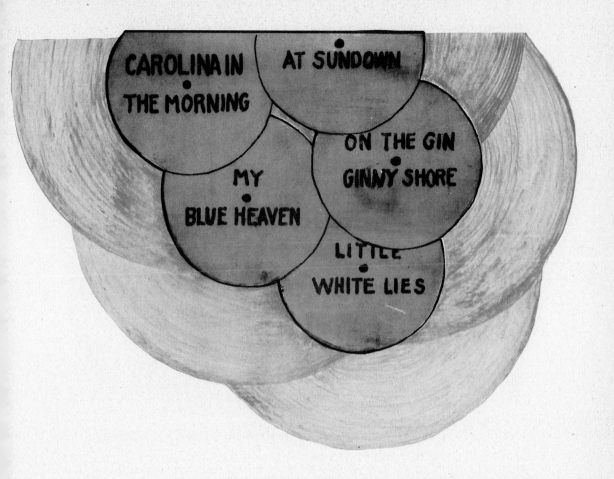

MUCH HAS BEEN SAID of the "high spirits" which typify jazz music and jazz dancing to so many. Yet no less an authority than Paul Whiteman is on record for its sad undertones. "I think it is a mistake to call jazz cheerful," he says. "It's the optimism of the pessimist who says, let's eat, drink and be merry for tomorrow we die. This cheerfulness of despair is quite American. . . Behind the rush of achievement is a restlessness of dissatisfaction, a vague yearning for something undefinable, beyond our grasp . . That is the thing expressed by that 'blues' chord, behind all the surface clamor and rhythm and energy of jazz." Whiteman's leap into social psychology is well worth considering. Certainly jazz comes out of a race whose lot was not happy. Transformed into cosmopolitan white culture, it was somewhat denuded of its primitivity and taken up more or less unconsciously as a means of drowning out the peacetime disillusionment that followed the madness of war. Hot jazz, featuring banjo and trumpet vied with sweet jazz of the piano and sax. Both combinations sold records galore.

GEORGE GERSHWIN was one of the greatest experimentalists Tin
Pan Alley has ever known. Taking courage from the success of his
early *Swanee*, he swam quickly into the full stream of jazz composition,
gave it new body and stature with an interplay of rhythms around,
above and under the melody. This is shown in *Fascinating Rhythm*, from
the musical Lady Be Good and also in *Strike Up The Band*. Working
tirelessly at his piano, Gershwin developed a jazz form which is technically called "rhythmic counterpoint." Those who are not experts
recognize the hidden lilt given a melody by impact of a triple (3/4)
rhythm in one hand against a double (4/4) rhythm in the other. With
Gershwin, jazz came a long ways from its primitive beginnings, was
now ready for the concert stage. That first concert was given by Paul
Whiteman and his band in Aeolion Hall on the afternoon of February
12, 1924. It made history, established a new art form. The trumpet
took over from the less esthetic cornet, cavorted sweetly over the
breaks. New arrangements provided relief from brassy blowing.
Whiteman was first leader to insist on a definite *note* in jazz improvisation, so that a piece was played more or less the same way twice in
succession. He and Gershwin made a great team.

[74]

Rhapsody In Blue

NO ONE WHO HAS HEARD Paul Whiteman's band open a Gershwin concert needs any introduction to the all-time great of jazz. In *Rhapsody In Blue*, Tin Pan Alley took a place among the immortals

JAZZ, THE WANTON, was only partly responsible for the scrapping of old dances. World War I, just ending, had developed a new freedom from convention. Even the one-step and the Castle Walk—first timid invitations to enter into the more abundant social life—lacked the proper energy release. The tune which blessed the transformation to jazz is an almost forgotten something called *Too Much Mustard*. It was as near to nothing at all as much can be, but pounded out a 4/4 rhythm with a persistence that cancelled conventions. Then followed the welding of the fox trot and the negro's blues songs. From Deep South chants to Manhattan Jazz tunes was quite a step and required

the best of the best composers of the era. First, the misplaced accent, the emphatic beat anticipated or delayed so as not to coincide with the basic beat of the dance, was used to stress some word or thought in the singer's lament. Second, the missing beat was used to challenge dancers to fill in with motions all their own. Third, there was the harmonic innovation, a flatted seventh, enabling the composer to put special emphasis in such lines as "Can't Help Loving That *Man* Of Mine". Finally, there was the long break between lines—an opening for orchestral improvisation and a precurser of "swing." The most astonishing part of the titles recorded above is the fluidity of the music.

PERIOD SONGS occasionally get anchored to period personalities. Among women, Marilyn Miller was one of a triumvirate to capture 1920's fancy; wholesomely sweet, she stood for contrast with the delicious wickedness of Clara Bow, "It" girl of the movies, and Gilda Grey, renowned shimmy dancer. Marilyn Miller died young, still lives on in the hearts of many who sing "*Peter Pan* I love you, loved you from the start." [78]

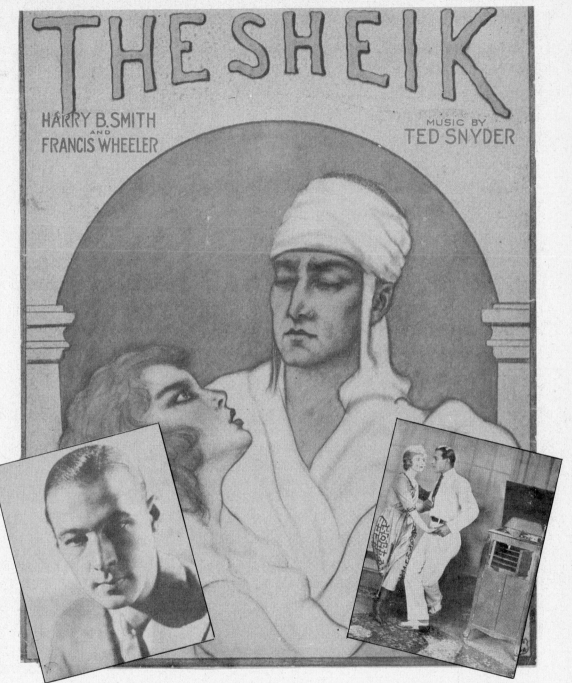

THE SHEIK

HARRY B. SMITH
AND
FRANCIS WHEELER

MUSIC BY
TED SNYDER

RUDOLPH VALENTINO came upon the screen in dashing foreign costume, danced the tango devinely and bent women back from the waist to kiss them. In darkened movie houses millions of female worshippers felt his breath of pure passion, yearned to cast the American male in his image. But the average Joe gave a rather unconvincing rendition of "I'm the Sheik of Araby, your love belongs to me. Each night when you're asleep, into your tent I'll creep." [79]

PERIOD ADVERTISEMENT indicating the twin gods of the dance-mad world, the sax and the phonograph. The background music, quite fittingly, is from *Whispering*, top foxtrot tune of its day.

DECADE OF PROHIBITION, "the noble experiment", that did not work. People flocked to speakeasies and blind pigs for wine, women and song. Night club was born, Texas Guinin's slogan, "hello, sucker."

THOSE WHO WERE THERE may possibly recapture the zany gaiety of the 20's in such songs as *Yes, We Have No Bananas, Singing In The Rain, It Ain't Gonna Rain No More* and *Breezin' Along With The Breeze.* Tin Pan Alley guessed wrong on Prohibition. They thought more people would spend more time at home around the piano and buy more sheet music. Instead blind pig's flourished. All of the songs whose covers are pictured here have a hootchy-kootchy rhythm and were considered "hot stuff" in their day. How many unexpurgated choruses to *Singing In The Rain* and *Button Up Your Overcoat* yet remain is memory's gamble.

BEST visual cue to the bygone careless days and happy hours is provided by John Held, Jr's. flapper, shown proposing a liquor toast to the sentiments expressed in *Button Up Your Overcoat*. Held intended such pictures as satire, found that flaming youth copied **them**.

HEY, HEY, FARMER GRAY, TOOK ANOTHER LOAD AWAY..."

[84]

THE UKELELE AND THE NOVELTY SONG were inveterate companions in the 1920's. Practically every song sheet carried an "Ukelele arrangement", simple dot diagrams to show finger position required for harmonizing chords. Songs like those shown above were most popular with the flappers and their boy friends. It was lots of fun and did not take much voice to sing, *Why Did I Kiss That Girl*, *If You Knew Susie, Like I Know Susie*, and dozens of others. Perhaps the most typical novelty song is the one shown on the opposite page, with its innumerable verses—and many impromptu additions, each ending with the chorus "Oh, the farmer, the farmer, took another load away.

[85]

VIENNESE TYPE OF OPERETTA had its swan song in the 1920's. But what a swan song it was! Sigmund Romberg's *Blossom Time* and *Student Prince*, and Rudolph Friml's *Rose Marie* and *The Vagabond King* led the parade. Above are song covers and personalities from these shows. Ilse Marvenga, the original Kathie, is shown against the Student's drinking song; Macie Worth is shown as she sang the Romberg music built around the story of composer Franz Shubert; Doris (*Indian Love Call*) Patston appears against a song cover from *Rose Marie*. On the opposite page is a theatre program from *The Vagabond King*, showing its star (Dennis King) and its songs. Both Romberg and Friml reached their top form in the 20's, are remembered for several other scores besides those indicated here. Who can ever forget *The Desert Song* or *One Kiss* and *Lover Come Back To Me*, from Romberg's operetta *The New Moon*. Friml classics include "*I Need Sy-m-pa-thy* (from The Firefly) and *L'amour-Tourjours-L'amour*. Like l'amour, such songs are everlasting. Radio and screen personalities also participated in the popularization of operetta in the decade. Jeannette MacDonald and Nelson Eddy, together or apart, led the parade back to the old favorites Naughty Marietta, Merry Widow and The Chocolate Soldier.

[86]

Song of the Vagabonds

Come all ye beggars of Paris Town,
  Ye lousy rabble of low degree—
We'll spare King Louis to keep his crown
  And save our city from Burgundy.
You and I are good for nothing but to die—
  Let us die for liberty!

CHORUS

Sons of toil and danger, will you serve a stranger
  And bow down to Burgundy?
Sons of shame and sorrow, will you cheer tomorrow
  For the crown of Burgundy?
Onward! Onward! swords against the foe!
  Forward, forward the lily banners go!
Sons of France around us, break the chain that bound us,
  And to hell with Burgundy!

Dennis King

Only A Rose

Red rose out of the east,
Tell the love I love least—who knows?
Red rose out of the west,
Tell the love I love best, "Love is a Rose."

CHORUS

Only a rose—I give you,
Only a song—dying away,
Only a smile—to keep in memory,
Until we meet—another day.
Only a rose to whisper—
Blushing as roses do.
I'll bring along a smile or a song for anyone,
Only a rose—for you.

8

Lips that spoke_ of kiss - ing)

We shall meet _____

HOT JAZZ. After-war hysteria demanded a new release and a new sensitivity. Drown the cares of the world in noise, roll in sexy rhythm; —hot jazz. Sooth the wound of the world in soft insinuation, tempt and titilate;—sweet jazz. And both in the service of the great god Aphrodisia. Above are shown three "hot" numbers: Helen Kane's (boop-boop-a-doop girl) *That's My Weakness Now*, Fred Fisher's *Dardanella*, and *I Wanna Go Where You Go* which features a picture of Ethel Waters. Try dancing any one of these to a hot band's rendition and you will quickly experience the urge to excess muscular exertion, the stimulus to work yourself into a frenzy. Such dancing came naturally to the less inhibited negro. That is why famed Ethel Waters, who danced in the 1920's with increditable vigor, was billed as "hot jazz incarnate."

(Lone-ly lips

Still in dreams, I hear you say,

SWEET JAZZ. Equally derivative from the original negro blues, the three songs pictured above are in the tradition of sweet jazz. Irving Berlin's *Crinoline Days*, Vincent Youmans' *More Than You Know* and *Sweetheart Of All My Dreams*, which features a picture of Adele Astair. All of these tunes can be danced with grace and delicacy. Paul Whiteman, in his historic concert of 1924, showed what could be done with the brasses singing instead of shouting, with the strings melting into the general ensemble rather than trying to maintain a rival organization. The special color of sweet jazz came from the saxophone, which took over from the violin of the old-time dance orchestra. With it all went a sophisticated restraint, typified by the dancing of Adele Astaire, who was once called "the high-priestess of sweet jazz.'

[89]

AL JOLSON, greatest of all the mammy singers, shown here with Swannee, the song which vaulted him into stardom, and *My Mammy*, the song which fixed him permanently in the heavens . . . Psychologists will tell you that the appeal of such songs lies in the child that remains in every man. No matter how worldly and adult we may become, there are times when we'd all like to escape our problems and responsibilities, turn back in memory to sing "I was a baby mammy, cooing on your knee, and mighty soon dear mammy, that's where I'll be." Mammy songs may not be as beautiful as some of the earlier mother songs, but their uninhibited expressions of sentiment were what the 20's wanted.

[90]

BLACKFACE MAMMY ACT of Al Jolson's stopped the show
SIMBAD and set other performers down the golden road to mammy
singing. Best known is Eddie Cantor and his "*I Want My Mammy,*
little old fashioned mammy, just to rock me to sleep when the night
shadows creep." Other well known performers of the day are shown
here on the covers of such song hits as *No One Loves You Better Than
Your M-A-double M-Y,* the rollicking "*I'm Alabamy Bound,* I'll have
no hebee jebees hanging round, just hear that choo-choo sound, I know
we're goin' to cover mammy ground," the plaintive "*Carolina Mammy,* I'm longing for you." Period Piece among mammy singers was
Karyl Norman and her *Don't Leave Me Dear Old Mammy.* [91]

THE ZIEGFELD FOLLIES, which began running in 1907, had by now reached rip-tide. Never were the productions more lavish, the girls more scantily clad or the tickets more exhorbitantly priced than in the lush 20's. The dandified impressario had finally lost his original label of "Anna Held's husband" (and Anna, too). Instead, he "glorified the American girl," owned the leading playhouse on Broadway and produced musical comedies as well as his Follies revue. One of the best Ziegfeld musicals from the standpoint of song content was *Whoopee*, featuring Eddie Cantor and Ruth Etting. 'Whoopee' was also typical of the behavior practiced by thousands of out-of-towners, who sated themselves on New York fleshpots in this roaring, flamboyant decade.

[92]

MY MAN (**MON HOMME**)

Fannie Brice's Famous Character Song

FANNIE
BRICE

PUBLISHED IN AMERICA BY LEO. FEIST, INC., FE

FANNIE BRICE AND HER SONG. The famous commedienne is known to today's youngsters as Baby Snooks. But millions still remember her, "Oh, my man I love him so he'll never know; all my life. . ."

PERIOD PIECE. Three ballad foxtrots that young love enjoyed singing together. Can *you* hear them? "*Sposing* I should fall in love with you, do you think that you could love me too," "I am a broken heart, *Among My Souvenirs*" on down to "He looks like you, he looks like me, he looks like me, He's everything we'd like him to be, that's Junior. . . our *Junior*."

[94]

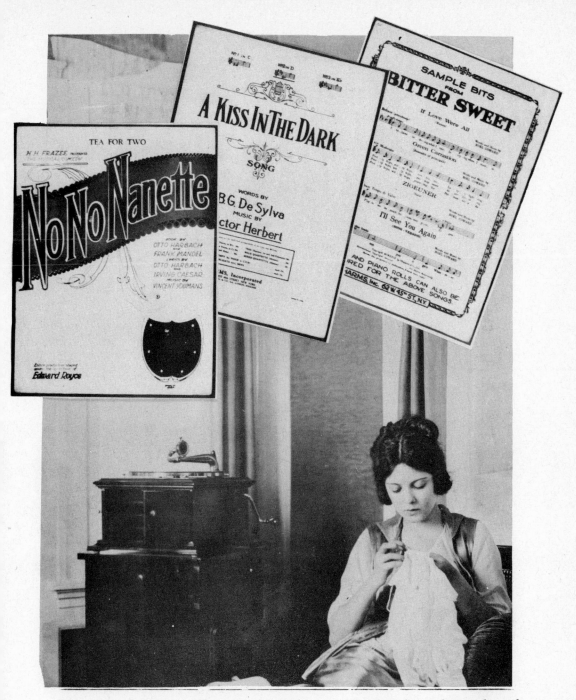

PERIOD PIECE. The phonograph, now passing into the realm of collectors' items, is ready to pour out such dreamy favorites as Openshaw's *Love Sends A Little Gift Of Roses*, Herbert's *A Kiss In The Dark* and Youmans' inimitable *Tea For Two*. Shown also are the song publishers' "sample bits" from *Bittersweet*, the Noel Coward musical which showed him to be as good a tunesmith as a playright.

[95]

ZIEGFELD THEATRE
54th STREET and SIXTH AVENUE
Matinee Thursday and Saturday

Music by
JEROME KERN

Based on the novel by
EDNA FERBER

PEOPLE WILL ARGUE always about the best musical show, depending upon individual memories. But when you come to "best" in terms of expert opinion and universal appeal, there are few contenders to Show Boat. Both from the standpoint of musical score and the sweep of the story, here was a great 'great.' Prime honor, of course, goes to Jerome Kern, whose SHOW BOAT songs have been sung and whistled by millions. A show built on Edna Ferber's great novel of a passing American institution, it completely violated the formula for girl and music shows, went contrary to all musical comedy tradition. Broadway was horrified. Yet this folk opera, first staged in 1927, had everything, including a fabulous cast pictured by Nell Brinkley on accompanying pages. Here was Kern at his brilliant best. Here was perfection. Its universal appeal was best expressed by Edna Ferber: "As the writing of the play Show Boat proceeded . . . I heard the score by bits and pieces . . . I had thrilled at *Can't Help Lovin' Dat Man* with its love-bemused lyric. I had melted under the bewitching strains of *Make Believe* and *Why Do I Love You?* And then Jerome Kern appeared late one afternoon with a strange look of exaltation in his eyes. He sat down at the piano. He didn't play the piano particularly well and his singing voice, though true, was negligible. But the music of *"Ol' Man River,"* mounted, mounted, until I breathed like a heroine in a melodrama. This was great music. This music would outlive Kern's day and mine."

[96]

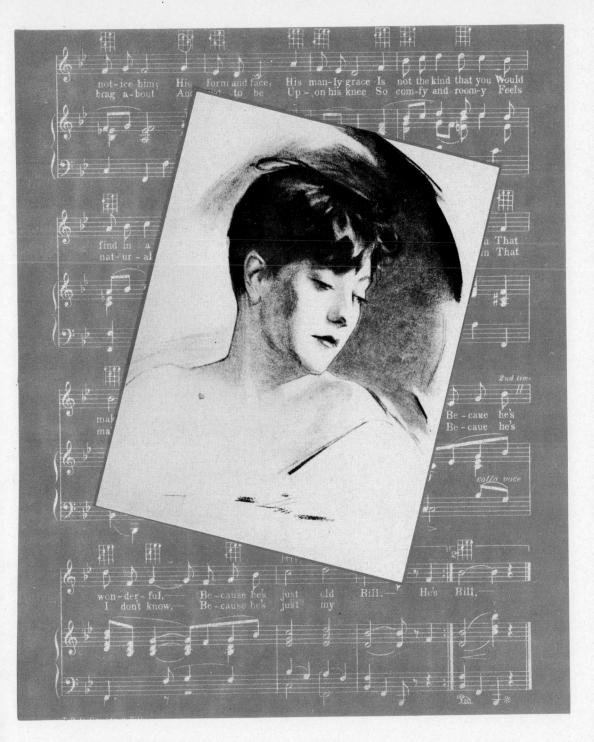

ONLY OCCASIONALLY does a song get forever tied to a particular singer, as is the case of Helen Morgan, sitting on her piano in Show Boat and singing *Just My Bill*. She began her "moanin' " in a Chicago cabaret, made her way to stage via George White's Scandals.

By NELL BRINKLEY

"Show Boat" is certainly "Ziegfeld's Show Boat," as it is labelled on Broadway, and more significantly, off it. For no one else in this town or any country outside it, has a "show," an entertainment, or, to reluctantly put it in the species of entertainment that I reckon it's supposed to belong in, a musical comedy, distantly related to it in beauty and excellence, and differentness. Musical comedy it is, perhaps, yes. Only this is a musical TRAGEDY, —AND a comedy.

It has beauty, as all the Ziegfeld shows have. But the genius behind it THIS time has come out in a musical show so different from all the others that it revives the musical-comedy-weary one, and gives him the long-stranger tickle of being glad he spent his money for his seats. The writer and the gentleman she is closely related to haven't felt glad in that particular way, when the spent-upon was musical and comedy, in a long time! And they were both losing hope entirely of getting any more thrills out of such and falling off in their attendance—unless there were TAP DANCERS. And you can't exist, theatrically, on them, however good.

Then along came SHOW BOAT! With a name that invited and inveigled. With beauty. Life. Tenderness. Perfect cleanness of line and comedy. Pep. Perfect comedy that tickles the very last rib—that's the hard one you know. New—in direction and atmosphere. Delightful music. And—eighth wonder of the musical entertainment stage—a story as enthralling as the book or movie you ever wept and laughed over! A real plot, a plot that you care about. With beauty and sweetness and an awful heartache, and lots of merry-merry!

Two things I cannot believe you ever heard of before in a "show." A story that begins, progresses and ends, and that makes you care whether it does or not, unlike the usual frail plots that sparkle a moment and then get lost like a desert stream that sinks in the sand and nobody knows just where it did it. Two things. An actual story and real tragedy. You never did. I never did. And the gentleman in front of me—seems HE never did. For he said so. Using his handkerchief, trumpet-like, he said to the lady beside him: "This is the first time in my life that I ever wept at a musical comedy, or got really interested in whether the lovely lady got her man. And I see I have company—plenty."

It would be a doubtful deed to tell you, if you don't know, the story, the settings, the atmosphere of humor, excitement, and drama, what fun is, that goes on, where its newness lies, of the very best show in New York. Better let you get it brand new, as I did.

"SHOW BOAT" is the perfect amusement. Itself perfect and perfectly offered. Every one in it is so fine that we sadly own to not knowing our own minds about a choice. If we did so, we might say, Eva Puck and Edna May Oliver. And then would arise to tor-

Helen Morgan.

Ziegfeld Blos[s]

Charles Winninger. as "Cap'n Andy."

Edna May Oliver. "Parthy Ann."

"Helen Morgan as 'Julie'" SINGING "CAN'T HELP LOVIN' THAT MAN."

On the "Cotton Blossom."

Norma Terris.

Sammy White. "Frank"

Eva Puck. "Ellie"

Norma Terris as "Magnolia."

Jules Bledsoe, singing "Old Man River"

Marsh and Eleanor Shaw "Kim"

ment us with her face and her song, that is as the face and the singing of Eve and Cleopatra, so universal and of no time and place is her beauty, Helen Morgan. And then the old-time beauty of Norma Terris. And then the artist, Charles Winninger; and the sincere comedian, Sammy White. And the voice of Howard Marsh. And we'd be back where we starated, smacking our hands together for EVERYBODY is "Show Boat."

And not forgetting the colored folks! Their voices will sing in your dreams
"Fish gotta swim,
Bird gotto fly,
Ah gotta love
One man 'till ah die."

JEROME KERN is often called the first of the great innovationists in popular music. One of the few composers with a first rate musical education, Kern early began to experiment with a long melodic line, three-part harmony and breath-taking jumps. Before the 20's, he had arrived with *They Didn't Believe Me;* but his highest achievements are of this decade. Working with Oscar Hammerstein II, Buddy DeSilva and other lyricists, he turned out a stream of tunes that will live forever. First there was *Sally.* with Marilyn Miller singing *Look For The Silver Lining.* This was followed by Sunny with its haunting "*Who* stole my heart away, who makes me dream all day, who...who...no one but you." People had begun to think of Marilyn as an exclusive Kern artist, for she did handle his melodies superbly. Then came his Show Boat, and after that the score for Sweet Adaline, with songs like *Why Was I Born* written especially for the moaning voice of Helen Morgan and other singers, as shown in the period sketch on the opposite page.

KERN went to Hollywood in 1934 and spent last years of life turning out slick scores based mainly on his earlier show successes. Only in *Smoke Gets In Your Eyes* and *The Way You Look Tonight* did he measure up fully to the tunes memoralized on this page.

[100]

Glimpses from the Wings of
"Sweet Adeline"

Arthur Hammerstein's Musical Rejuvenation of the Mauve Decade

The lady in the upper corner with the leg-of-mutton sleeves is Irene Franklin, looking somewhat doubtfully at Robert Emmet Keane who sports the correct Brooks Brothers ensemble for the gay nineties. Just below, Robert Chisholm discusses life, letters, and Hoboken (the scene of the piece) with Helen Morgan, while at the right, Charles Butterworth gazes complacently upon the charming

TALKING PICTURES did not make the theme song; they simply capitalized what was latent in the pattern of current movie entertainment. In the late 1920's there was hardly a theatre of any pretensions without its pipe organ. While there was less for the organist to do, now that the song was on the sound track, his incessant repetition of the theme before and after the main feature helped drive home the melody and send the customers out to buy sheet music. Above are two of the outstanding theme songs of the late 20's, published by the music subsidiary of Metro-Goldwyn-Mayer, and credited roughly with having more than half the hit tunes from movies in its portfolio. The percentage of "flops" in picture-songs was very high and music dealers learned to be wary of them. They tended to favor a free-lance publication which was not dinned to death in the movies. Yet there are few songs of the period which have stood up so well as Broadway Melody's

PIPES OF A MODERN PAN. "The increasing popularity of the organ as a secular instrument is seen in this picture of a recent theatre installation." Thus did newspaper announce era of movie theme song.

MEMENTOES from the theme song area. In the 1920's movie going
had become standard entertainment for all America. What leisure
time was not taken with the phonograph and dancing was spent in the
vicarious satisfactions of the silver screen. Luxurious palaces were built
to take care of the multitudes; and toward the end of the decade, when
the public's taste for shadow love-making was somewhat satiated, along
came the sound track. Celluloid heroes and heroines took on new life
and body as they talked and sang. The first Vitaphone program was
presented on Broadway in the Warner Brothers Theatre in 1926. De-
ficient both technically and esthetically, effect was still electric.
[104]

THREE GREATS among early sound movie's. These made history. First came *Seventh Heaven*, so closely identified with its love waltz, *Diane*, that millions went from the show to hum, dance or sing "I'm in heaven when I see you smile—my Diane, . . ." Equally popular was song by the same writers, "I wonder why you keep me waiting, *Charmaine*—cries in vain." Everyone knows, of course, that Al Jolson "made" the vitaphone big time, singing "When there are grey skies, I don't mind the grey skies, you made them blue, *Sonny Boy*." But for setting a new form, many authorities pay their respects to *Sunny Side Up*. Here was a show-song combination that had everything; Janet Gaynor —the epitome of all wishful shopgirls in the land, finding her heart's desire in millionaire Charles Farrell and singing her joys in *I'm a dreamer, aren't we all*, and *Keep Your Sunny Side up, up.* This movie was also to be remembered for the gay fantasy dance number, "*Turn on the heat*, start in to strut, wiggle, wobble and warm up the hut", and "*If I had a talking picture of you-oo*, I would run it whole night through-oo." In this end-of-decade show technical difficulties were finally ironed out. Here at last was fully consumated the wedding of screen and phonograph, the perfect union of sight and sound.

[105]

UNDERNEATH THE
MELLOW MOON

By WENDELL W HALL
"The Singing Xylophonist"

WENDELL HALL, "the singing xylophonist", wrote many a popular song, but none with more staying power than his dreamy *Underneath The Mellow Moon*. Dancers still call for it.

[106]

THE DANCE WORLD has never seen anything like it before or since. From the deep south straight to Manhattan for high-styling went *The Charleston*, titalating dance duo to stop all others. Cover is original.

HIGH SOCIETY and Manhattan's tango-tea crowd were well up on dancing before the 20's, but not until phonograph records became widely distributed did the dance craze hit all America. Never did the human drumstick get so exercised. Above are three dance tunes that flaming youth will never forget.

Dance bands were now beginning to acquire reputations. As wine cellars were outlawed and cusine declined, people no longer mentioned the name of a restaurant, but said they were going to dance to Ted Lewis or Ray Miller, playing "*Wat you going to do to whet your whistle* and *Everybody's got a key to my cellar.*"

One of the great dance song writers of the period was Richard E. Whiting, father of radio songstress, Margaret Whiting. With a succession of lyric writers, he turned out such hits as *Japanese Sandman* (1920), *Ain't We Got Fun* (1921), *Sleepy Time Gal* (1924), *Ukelele Lady* (1925), *Horses* (1926), *She's Funny That Way* (1928), *Louise* (1929), and *Beyond the Blue Horizon* (1930). Whiting was a serious student of what makes a song popular and frequently lectured his younger collaborators on choice of words and title phrase. "The word *Cherie*" he said, "should put any song across." To this a collaborator once proposed a never written item entitled "I Can't Get to Tucson, Too Soon, Cherie."

FIVE WALTZES from the 1920's. It is interesting to find that even during the period of unrivaled interest in new dance steps, this tried and true dance step was not forgotten. The younger set maintained that the custom of making every other dance a waltz was out of deference to old folks, who thought the Tango and Fox Trot awful, and the Charleston, Black Bottom and Nigger Itch downright immoral. But youngsters were observed to enjoy the waltzes almost as much as their parents. The reason is that 3/4 time, with its rest third beat, is the most natural dance time, according to authorities. Note the prominence of "moon songs"; the waltz was a good number to stop on, and "moon" suggested "spoon."

[109]

OUR PREOCCUPATION with the phonograph-fox-trot mania of the '20s has not obscured another and cognate song developments. Considerable influence came from the movies, especially with the introduction of the sound track. Even in the days of silents, movie houses had made considerable use of popular songs; played by the ever-present pianist, these were woven into background music suggestive of the mood appropriate to the pictures shown. But this was second-hand material, as such contributed nothing new to popular song. Not until the movie makers sought to lure customers back into their darkened halls by sound films, were highly creative song talents put to work. And even with the best of musical movies, you could only say that the composers were very highly paid to turn out songs they might have written anyway, quite without the golden flood. The sound movies moved a great deal of song-writing talent from New York to Hollywood, left their product pretty much as it already was. As a vehicle for popularizing a song, movie theme songs had distinct disadvantages. Whereas the phonograph record could be played occasionally and at will, Theme-song rendition often dinned the tune out of memory by overrepetition. For example, if there was an auto accident in the picture, you would probably find the hero rescuing the heroine while bellowing, "You're the Cream in My Coffee." In the next scene, a hospital interne would reprise the same number to a pretty nurse. And all the time the heroine was on the operating table, "You're the Cream in My Coffee" would be heard as background music. And if this were not enough, you could confidently expect to hear it again, as the heroine did a switcheroo and fell in love with the surgeon. In the end she might marry either surgeon or original hero: It made no difference, singing "You're the Cream in my Coffee."

1930

Music in the Air . . .

1930 FOUND AMERICA recovering from a daze. In one swoop, the stock market crash of the previous October had snuffed out most of Flaming Youth's fire. It was fashionable, of course, to spoof at the new poverty. "*Brother, can you spare a dime*" and "*What to do about it? Let's turn out the lights and go to bed*" were the songs of the hour. The musicomedy *Face the Music* headlined "*I say it's spinach and to hell with it* as the theme-song of the Depression. Musically, however, it was not bad times that mattered in the 1930's, but rather radio's coming of age. Mr. and Mrs. J. Q. Public; already trained to prefer the recorded music of professionals to what they could make themselves, found the radio the ultimate in easy listening. No flipping of phonograph records, no cranking-up of the machine, no high-priced movie ticket. Just tune the dials of your radio receiver, sit back in your easy chair and let the melody float in. It was an era fascinated with MUSIC IN THE AIR.

In popular song, the transition from participant to spectator behavior was now almost complete. What the player-piano, the phonograph and the sound-movie had started, the radio all but finished. Pianos could be had for moving charges out of storage. Music and singing teachers had a permanent depression. Sheet music sales, which had sunk from the millions to the thousands when hit by the phonograph record, now seemingly went into a final tailspin. One publisher, in fact, proposed that no more sheets be issued for popular consumption, that compositions be placed only with professionals. ASCAP, guardian of the performance rights for composers and publishers, girded itself for battle with the new Goliath of mechanized music.

The public's love for radio was by no means confined to its novelty. It stemmed partly from the sprightly new tunes that were aired by a fascinating new group of celebrities. In the experimental 1920's, radio had no network programs and seldom paid for talent. Usually the employees of a plant that manufactured radios put on programs for benefit of the few who had sets on which to listen. By the 1930's, the advertising hucksters had discovered the new media, put high-priced talent on the air and won the public's ear.

[113]

FROM PHONOGRAPH TO RADIO. 1930 brought to a head a smoldering conflict between vehicles of song-plugging and named, as winner, the radio broadcast. The songs whose covers appear on this page were vaulted into popularity not by the record makers, not by the movies and vaudevillians, but by name-bands and singers who took to the airways. Phonograph records sales of hit tunes dropped from the millions to a hundred thousand copies. Some companies went broke. Publishers, who had come to rely upon substantial royalties from movies in need of "theme" songs, now found this source of revenue drying up. The public put their talking machines in the attic and stayed away from the movies in droves. The only way that the depression-ridden animals could be driven back in the theatres was by presenting personal appearances of radio personalities and name bands.

THE GENERATION born in the broadcast era recognizes this picture. Every studio had at the beginning its own orchestra for filling in between regularly sponsored programs with the popular songs of the day. Few will remember the songs they played for they were literally played to death. Not until a decade later did radio stations discover the financial virtues of replacing orchestras with disc jockeys.

[114]

A STUDY IN CONTRASTS: How far we come in so short a time.
At the beginning of the decade many listeners were getting their songs
over a receiver like that shown in the upper picture. By decades end,
the radio had become a streamlined affair. So, indeed, had the charac-
ters who listened and danced to the music. Styles in song changed too!

[115]

UP THROUGH THE 1900's, all melody for popular songs were arbitrarily confined to a range of an octave. The accompaniment went teum-ti-tium, and you knew exactly what was coming the next bar. Musical schools offered to teach all the chords (there were only four) needed for barbershop harmony in ten easy lessons. Today it takes a trained musician to play popular music. What made the difference? Partly, the despised saxophone. It annoyed listeners out of set musical expectancies and made a raucous nuisance of itself. People were obliged to forget what ought to be and to expect anything. Secondly, phonograph and radio (which presented trained singers in a counterattack on home singing) favored songs covering a range of one and one half octaves. Thirdly, there was the influence of modern harmonic

theory, its use of halftones for new color effects. Finally and most important of all, there was the entry into the popular field of gifted and imaginative composers with fine musical training. The daddy of these all was Jerome Kern, whose use of the altered chord, parallel fifth and delayed resolution, had been called daring in the 1920's and was now accepted form. But now Kern started to run two or three melodies together. Someone has remarked there is a greater difference between early and late Kern than between Shubert and the Strauss waltzes. Like most of his younger contemporaries of the 1930's, Kern was a trained student of musical theory striving for new rhythmic and melodic effects. That is why his song "Why was I born, why do I try now", stands head and shoulders above any of the very satisfactory compositions whose covers are shown above.

[117]

HIGH RIDING TUNE of the airways. Hoagy Carmichael's *Stardust* leads year after year in orchestra popularity counts. Even Tommy Dorsey's theme song, *Getting Sentimental Over You*, cannot match in pull.

AMONG BAND LEADERS of the period, Guy Lombardo and his Royal Canadians have a deserved niche. Playing "The sweetest music this side of heaven," they are still popular dance favorites.

THREE GREAT FAVORITES with radio listeners. Bing Crosby, Jimmie Durante and Bob Hope. If the three, Crosby had the best voice, a deep relaxed melodious baritone which brought him to the top of radio popularity polls year after year. Though never a crooner in the Rudy Vallee tradition, 'der Bingle' won almost equal admiration and support from young as well as old. Jimmy (Snozzle) Durante, the greatest low comedian of our day, had outgrown the night club circuit, was making movies like Palooka and featuring his own theme song *Inka Dinka Doo* over the air. Bob Hope was currently plugging a hit tune, *Two Sleepy People*, written by Hoagy Carmichael of *Stardust fame*.

THIS CHARMING French import seemed to have just the right accent, the right timing and the knowing, sophisticated wink to put a song across to a 1930 audience. Featured in sound movies and on the radio, Chavalier and his straw hat endeared hi.self to everyone. IMPORTANCE of radio performance for both publicity and profit was now well recognized by the song publishers and the radio artists. Radio listening had all but killed off sheet music sales, once figured in the millions, it took a lot of plugging even to get 100,000 copies sold. The piano virtually passed out of use and existence in the home. One could get a good one from almost any storage warehouse for the price of moving it away.

FIVE SONGS OF THE DEPRESSION. Always responsive to changing economic and social conditions, Tin Pan Alley outdid itself to sing away the blues of the hard times of the early 1930's. First and foremost of hit tunes was Ager and Yellen's *Happy Days Are Here Again*, soon used as the theme song of the victorious Democratic party. *Brother Can You Spare A Dime* brought the traditional tramps to the musical comedy stage. One of the most tuneful excursions into poverty appeared in *It's Only A Shanty In Old Shanty Town*. Walt Disney was also busily at work in battling the blues. From The Three Little Pigs comes *Who's Afraid Of The Big Bad Wolf* and from Snow White comes *Whistle While You Work*. [122]

ALMOST EVERYONE knows that Eddie Cantor grew up with radio. On the stage as one of Gus Edwards talented youngsters, later as a Ziegfeld Follies star, "Banjo Eyes" made his first appearance before the radio microphone in 1921. On Nov. 2, 1926, he made his first paid network broadcast over a group of stations that formed the nucleus of the National Broadcasting Company, and in 1931 he became star of the Chase and Sanborn hours, always signing off with his special "I'd love to spend" musical signature.

[123]

FORGOTTEN TUNES by three fine tunesmiths: Con Conrad, Gus Kahn and Peter De Rose *"Have you ever been lonely, have you ever been blue?"*. . . . . . . One of the outstanding contributions of this era's songs to popular music was the liberation of technical resourcefulness. In this song writers were helped out by advent of the phonograph and radio. In the first quarter of the century, ragtime and ballad numbers had to be tailored down to the capacities of the average high school girl and her singing boy friends. The melody dared not exceed an octave and the accompaniment had to be limited to the four principal chords in their most familiar positions. But with widespread public interest in radio, music no longer had to be made at home. Professional artists were encouraged to cart out their utmost tricks, including a two octave range, to dazzle the listeners. Likewise, skilled musicians were at liberty to compose harmonies and rhythms which only a professional could manage. Curiously enough, mechanical reproduction of music actually helped popular music to better, bolder things. Simultaneously there was also a development of sophistication in the lyrics of popular tunes; led by such stalwarts as Ira Gershwin, Buddy De Sylva, Gus Kahn, and Con Conrad, verses moved away from solid all-wood utterances of love and took a comedy line.

[124]

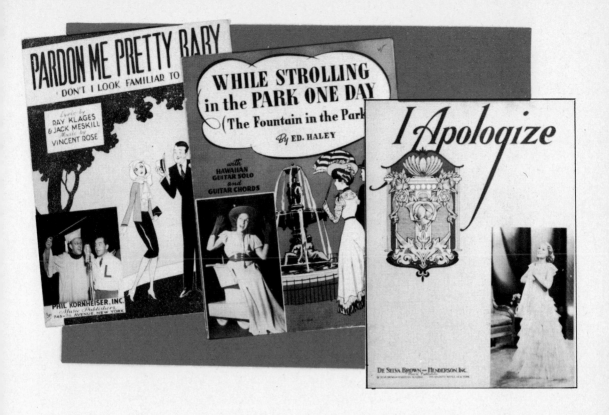

RADIO PRODUCED some fantastically successful song merchants in its years of coming of age. The songs they sang are not remembered so much as their manner of singing. Above are three personalities that have left their mark. Kay Kyser, and his Kollege of Musical Knowledge (here shown with John Meridith); also Connie Boswell. There was a time when Jessica Dragonette was the most popular singer in radio. She lived the part to the full, arriving at the studio with great fanfare, always sang in evening dress. The radio public felt a deep sense of personal attachment to this sweet-voiced singer. In the late 1930's, after a financial demonstration with her sponsors, Miss Dragonette retired from radio. Many of her fan clubs promptly announced they would boycott radio until she returned. She set out on a concert tour and attracted larger crowds than touring movie stars. In Minneapolis, fifteen thousand people ignored a taxi strike and a blizzard to hear her sing; in Chicago, one hundred and fifty thousand gathered in Grant Park for her summer concert. Such was fame.

Another great popular favorite, Connie Boswell, also made personal appearance tours throughout the land. Though paralyzed from the waist down, this radio star had a special cart made and used it on the stage with telling effect.

[125]

SERIOUS STUDENTS of the subject are always asking of popular song writers, "Can they write *music*." The disbeleivers will point out that some of the fabulously successful popular tunesmiths can hardly distinguish one note from another, much less know the intricacies of harmonic composition. It may be that early 19th century composers were often musically illiterate, but this could not be said of the majority who were writing themselves into popularity in the 1930's. Take composers like Gershwin, Porter, Kern, Swartz and Yellen as indicative of a trend. Their musicianship was much better than that of simple ballad writers, and they would not have lasted out the stock market crash if they had been simply interpreters of a bygone jazz age.

FIRST MUSICOMEDY to reach heights comparable to grand opera. Some, in fact, speak of George Gershwin's *Porgy And Bess* as the "finest American opera ever written." Above, we see the high spot of show, Todd Duncan singing to Anne Brown *Bess, you is my woman now.*

HERBERT PRIOR VALLEE, radio's earliest crooner, first star bandleader and pioneer producer, stands out as the greatest personality of the airways age. Infatuated with the saxophone as a boy, he taught himself to play and soon became an expert band performer. His soulful rendition of his own song, *Vagabond Lover*, was actually the first "crooning" ever heard over the air and brought a flood of inquiries. He now took the name of Rudy—Rudy Vallee. It sounded like Rudolph Valentino and he was soon to drive Valentino's wraith from feminine memories. Of the newcomer some analyst said "By divine accident or miracle, the voice that starts its strange journey at the microphone hardly more than banal fills the air at its destination with that rarest charm of beauty—uniqueness, novelty." His voice was a new sound and his sponsorship was the most sought after hallmark in Tin Pan Alley.
[128]

STEIN SONG

(UNIVERSITY OF MAINE)

A New Arrangement by RUDY VALLÉE

for

VOICE AND PIANO

Music by

E. A. FENSTAD

Arrangement by

A. W. SPRAGUE

Words by

LINCOLN COLCORD

Also Published

Vocal Orchestration
Special Dance Orchestration
Band Arrangement

CARL FISCHER, INC.
. . . . Cooper Square, NEW YORK

MEMORIAL to a great song and a great popularizer. *The Stein Song* was first written as a march in 1901. In 1910 it came to University of Maine. Vallee resurrected it during his freshman year there, brought it to radio via Yale and his Connecticut Yankees. Even today, people like to hear him tear through the song that was the motto of his age, "Drink to all the happy hours, drink to the careless days . . ."

THIS EAGER looking chap is the young Fred Waring, just out of college and about to be lured to the airways in the Old Gold show. Waring and his Pennsylvanians were connected with many song hits.

AMONG ORCHESTRA LEADERS, Paul Whiteman was still tops. On the radio he played sweet, rather than hot jazz. Paul was rapidly becoming the Dean of radio bandmen, gave many a new tune its boost.

GOD BLESS AMERICA was originally written by Sargeant Irving
Berlin for his all-soldier show of World War I, Yip, Yip, Yaphank.
First introduced to the public by Kate Smith on Armistice Day 1938.
[132]

FOREMOST LADY CROONER of her time rose to stardom in the early 1930's. Almost from her first broadcast, there was something wholesome, vital and real about Kate Smith and her singing. Originally billed as "The Songbird of the South," she soon became a national favorite. Her musical signature, *When The Moon Comes Over The Mountain,* will ever be associated with her voice and personality. But Kate Smith did much to center interest on other popular songs of the decade. She became among the most sought-after "pluggers" in the business. Her public's response to "Kate Smith Speaks" was nothing short of phenomenal. The most casual allusion to her birthday on the air would bring in a flood of presents. Her fan mail required several secretaries. Any product she spoke for was sure to have a substantial sale. But the social influence of this radio personality received its greatest test when, during World War II, Kate Smith undertook a marathon sale of war bonds. Over CBS, Miss Smith cajoled and pleaded with her audience off and on for 18 hours, pledged them to buy $39,000,000 worth. There could be no better demonstration of the badly exploited public's "Will to believe in a public figure thought to incarnate the virtues of sincerity, integrity, good fellowship and altruism."

[133]

THE SWING TO SWING. The hottest and best **kind of jazz** (according to connoisseurs) reached its golden age in the 1930's. Everyone called it Swing; but not even its most articulate advocates could give it strict definition. All agree that it is based on a driving, fluid and unmechanical rhythm over which soloists improvise as they play. This made jazz musically interesting and vital, and it permitted great musicians to develop their own unhampered style.

OFF-BEAT RHYTHM is as basic to swing as is melodic variety and improvisation. Every popular song can be swung, after some fashion. But numbers like the three above give a major break to the artists of swing. Gershwin's *Embraceable You*, whether played "sweet" or "hot", has a tantalizing rhythm that brings out the best in a good performer

[134]

SWING'S FIRST AGE of glory began around 1925 and focused around a negro trumpet player, Bix Beiderbecke, and recordings of hit *Hattie The Hustler* and *Minnie The Moocher*. Interest in this New Orleans-sparked jazz soon died out, was revived around 1934 with phenomenal success by Benny Goodman, Artie Shaw, Tommy Dorsey and other white bandmen. Swing, of course, has always been popular with negro jazz bands; its black royalty numbers, besides Bix Beider-becke, Joe (King) Oliver, the first to take New Orleans' rough street corner jazz and clean it up for general consumption, Louis (Prince) Armstrong, who learned form under Oliver, Edward (Duke) Elling-ton, leader, composer and arranger of such hits as *Mood Indigo*, and Bill (Count) Basie, a top-notch pianist whose *One O'Clock Jump* is a major classic. When all is said, however, about numbers which led the swing back to swing, the Oscar—by general consent—goes to *Stomping At The Savoy*, as played by Benny Goodman and the musicians shown. Swing did much to overlay the basic rhythm of the fox-trot with interesting sophisticated variation. Monotony of rhythm is the founda-tion of folk music, and the fox trot is the modern epitomy of the primitive urge to dance to insistent, monotonous rhythm. One thing Swing did was to make rhythm appeal to the head as well as to the feet.

[135]

THE SONGS a nation danced to came from a variety of sources; a foxtrot, *Body and Soul*, from a revue; a tango, *Flying Down To Rio*, from a movie; a "New York Walk", *You're My Everything*, from an Ed Wynn show.

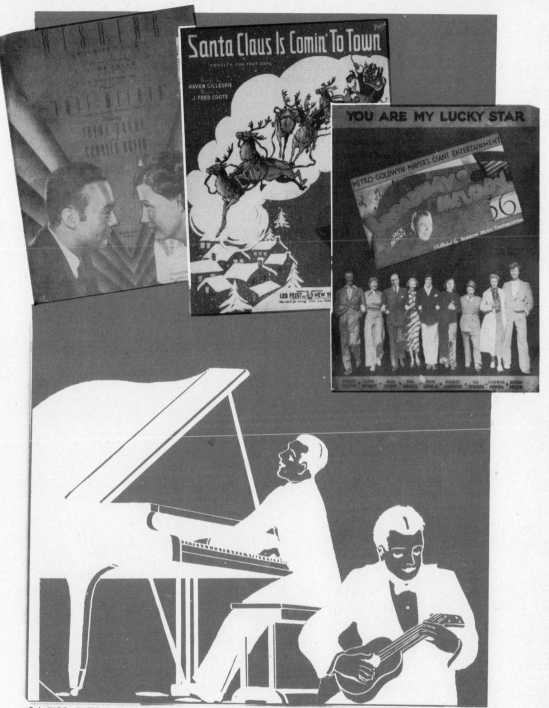

JACK BENNY'S Broadway Melody gave us *You Are My Lucky Star*, Irene Dunn and Charles Boyer first sang *Wishing Will Make It So*, while Jan Garber's orchestra plugged the novelty number, *Santa Claus Is Coming To Town*.

Time on my hands, You in my arms,
Nothing but love in view.

© 1930, VINCENT YOUMANS INC. AND MILLER
MUSIC CORP. ADAMSON AND GORDON WORDS

Love is sweeping the country,
Waves are hugging the shore.

© NEW WORLD MUSIC CORP.—1931

"OF THEE I SING," a Pulitzer prizewinning spoof
on politics, had this scene of a presidential candidate
campaigning with his ladylove. One of its songs by
George Gershwin was *Love Is Sweeping the Country.*

Just around the corner, there's a rainbow in the sky,
So let's have another cup o' coffee

© IRVING BERLIN, 1932

"FACE THE MUSIC," with songs by Irving Berlin, was put into production at the end of 1931 and
opened early in 1932. It made fun of a producer trying to raise money to put on a show during the depression. In its funniest scene impoverished New York so-
cialites, gathered for dinner at an Automat (*above*),
cheerfully accepted their fate by singing, *Let's have
another cup o' coffee, let's have another piece o' pie.*

LIFE MAGAZINE (Jan. 1, 1950) picked 1931 as Broadway's jackpot
year for great musical comedy songs. The page above memorilizes
three of the funniest, slickest song-and-dance shows ever written.

[138]

ABOVE is shown an early publicity shot of Ethel Merman, erstwhile private secretary, singing *I got Rhythm* in her break through to the big time. According to a contemporary account, "No one noticed (her) until, towards the end of the first act, leaning against a bar backdrop, she sent her voice in a slow wail, moaning, metallic and extraordinary, out over the heads of an audience whose attention had suddenly become electric." That is show business, with its overnight leap to fame.

RADIO BROADCASTING had come a long ways from its tiny beginnings in the 1920's; professional talent had replaced the amateurs recruited from the employees of Westinghouse, General Electric and other early operators of radio stations. Advertising agencies now placed stars under contract, bought the radio time and sold the "package" to some willing client with soap, toothpaste or cereals he wanted promoted over the air. Above are some of the top box-office performers in radio's showcase, and the songs they helped to popularize. *Shine On Harvest Moon*, introduced 20 years before by Nora Bayes, now became the radio signature of Ruth Etting, who left the Ziegfeld Follies for the more lucrative airways. Then there were the Boswell Sisters, most famous of the sisters acts that took to the microphone, singing what many regard as the greatest Jerome Kern melody, *Smoke Gets In Your Eyes*. Last, but by no means least, was Lanny Ross and his Show-Boat program. Kern's great musical comedy based on the Edna Ferber novel encouraged moviemakers to develop their own version, also radio show. The song, *Here Comes the Show Boat*, was first used in the movie, later became the musical signature of a radio variety show holding top "Hopperatings" throughout the 1930's.

THREE LITTLE WORDS (I Love You) was a smash hit song in 1935, and here are the three little girls who helped to put it over on the air.

IN STARS like Ethel Merman, Cole Porter songs found the type of robust personality and full blown manner of delivery precisely suited to their racy flavor. Some will recall Ethel yelling "Friendship, friendship, what a beautiful friendship" from Du Barry Was A Lady. Others will remember "It's delightful, it's delimit, it's deloverly"; and still others will recall her singing "I get a kick out of you" from Anything Goes. Other great Porter songs include *Night And Day*, *My Heart Belongs To Daddy* and the all-time favorite, *Begin The Beguine*. Porter approaches his favorite subject—love—in a slightly cynical vein. He is more often disillusioned than starry eyed, more often passionate than sweetly sentimental. International society lionized Cole Porter long before his songs caught on in public favor. In 1934 he wrote *You're The Top* and inspired a sort of cult of Cole Porter parodists. But no one was able to improve upon the stylistic grace, comic impudence and inuendo of such lines as, "You're the bangle I long to dangle."

When the movies decided to build a musical around Cole Porter's life, the scripters were stumped. "No struggle," they said, "man was born with silver spoon in his mouth." All the greater credit then, that this son-of-wealth deserved fame lacks a money drive.

[142]

COLE PORTER SONGS have been the darling of sophisticates ever since he got into trouble at prep school for writing off-color lyrics. Master of the double ententre text, Porter is, more importantly, a master of tantalizing tunes which, like love, get under your skin.

ONE HAS ONLY to look over the song folios of the period to recall the new school of "singing cowboys", who reached down to grasp something earthy and 'American' in their guitar-accompanied music.

COWBOY SONGS—or alleged ones—were beginning to come into popularity in the 1930's, did not reach rip-tide till a decade later. Above song became a perennial favorite, rivaling *Home On The Range*.

THE 1930's saw many new names among hit-tune writers, as well as some old standbys. Yellen and Ager led the parade with *Ain't She Sweet, Crazy Words, Crazy Tunes, I'm Waiting For Ships That Never Come In, I Wonder What's Become Of Sally*, and many another. Continental song hits, like *Two Heart's In 3/4 Time*, and *Auf Wiedersehen*, were given the American treatment. Everyone hummed and waltzed to *Auf Wiedersehen, My Dear*. Above are some songs of ageless appeal, also some that are already dated and forgotten. Walter Donaldson, whose *Little White Lies*, vaulted into the limelight during the 1920's was still writing hit tunes, including the never-to-be-forgotten "You, you're *driving me crazy* . . . what did I do? what did I do? My tear for you, make everything hazy, clouding the skies of blue." And who of that decade will forget Gershwin's "*Embrace Me, My Sweet Embraceable You.*" Jazz-music, in the '30's, was still being led to new heights of daity dizziness by the sure hand of Gershwin. Recall the variations permitted the performer by the long melodic break. The piano virtuoso interpolated rhythm and new harmonics; the professional singer made *sotte voce* comments on the subject of his discourse; the trap drummer exhibited his full dozen of gadgets and displayed his skill at juggling; the brass trumpeter got in a few 'hot licks' from his muted instrument.

[146]

SONG COVERS from the 7th, 8th and 9th editions of Earl Carroll's Vanities serve as reminders of a type of popular musical entertainment that had now reached rip-tide. Ziegfeld Follies saw their last days but Earl Carroll had built himself a new theatre with the following inscription over the stage door, "Through these portals pass the most beautiful girls in the world." People sometimes forget that these girly extravaganzas were often as closely linked to melody as to feminine pulchritude. Earl Carroll, "America's foremost authority on feminine beauty," was also a connoisseur in the matter of judging the potential qualities of a song. In the solitude of his studio or the darkness of his theatre, this master showman selected the music that later set millions of hearts pulsating, millions of toes tingling. The tune had to be tried out in various keys and tempos before he found the exact combination that would make its melody linger on,—a nation hum and whistle: "Once in a lifetime, someone comes along, bringing happiness for two" Another producer of the decade, George White and his Scandals, occasionally had hit tunes, but few to rival Carroll's and The Great Ziegfeld's. Yet all contributed to make the song and dance show an unique American contribution to the world of the stage.

[147]

$1,000,000 Worth of Radio Stars!*

Tune them all in on

WAAA CBS

000 on your dial

* This month alone, CBS Network programs bring you more tnan $1,000,00 worth of all-star radio talent. Tune in these headliners tonight on this statio

YOUR HIT PARADE 9:00 p. m. Frank Sinatra and Joan Edwards sing the top tunes of the week. Mark Warnow conducts; the Hit Paraders assist. The result is one of the nation's favorite programs.

KENNY BAKER 8:00 p. m. The top tenor greets his big name guests with a glad hand and glad song when they drop in for their regular Saturday night visits.

HOME SWEET HOME 123456789

SATURDAY NIGHT SERENADE 9:45 p. m. Jessica Dragonette fills the air with songs of yesterday, today and tomorrow. A serenade to suit all tastes and ages.

Tonight! THE BIGGEST SHOW IN TOWN

END OF THE DECADE. Radio personalities had become such an asset for pulling listeners that the two major broadcasting companies were embarked upon a talent auction that drove fantastic salaries even higher. The above advertisement tells, more than words, what had happened to the song world. Gone were the days of stage and vaudeville plugging. If any new melodies were to be put across (or old ones revived) it would be by aid of radio. "Your Hit Parade" capitalized the growing popularity of the bobby soxer's rave, Frank Sinatra. When he made personal theatre appearances they swooned in the aisle.

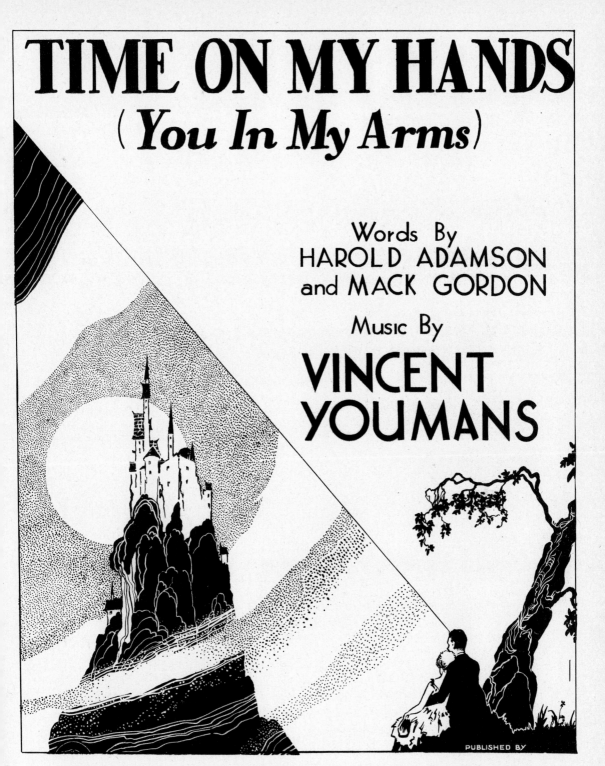

TIME ON MY HANDS
(*You In My Arms*)

Words By
HAROLD ADAMSON
and MACK GORDON

Music By

VINCENT YOUMANS

PUBLISHED BY

EYE OPENER for the decade. Languid new mood introduced by lonely new song writer. Vincent Youmans' "Time on my hands, you in my arms, nothing but love in view" made ideal cocktail music.

[149]

ON MOVIE LOTS, producers worked overtime to give a public made song conscious by the radio what it wanted in the way of musical comedy. Above are some of the "discoveries" of the 1930's. The fabulous team of Jeannette MacDonald and Nelson Eddy went through practically a whole cycle of Victor Herbert operettas adapted for the movie medium. Dick Powell popularized a whole cycle of old favorites in movies which exploited his fine voice and ability to play. Deanna Durbin was discovered when still in high school, rose to instant popularity on radio and screen. *Amapola* was only one of her starring pieces. Jeannette MacDonald served to revive the *The Merry Widow*, and Nelson Eddy to revive *The Chocolate Soldier*. [150]

SOUND MOVIES in the 1930's continued their inroads into the popular music field. Practically all the younger song writers had now migrated to Hollywood where for fabulous salaries, they dreamed up theme songs and tunes to help put a movie across. Above are five typical examples. Only one of these, *The Wizard of Oz*, made history. A fine story of fantasy, blest with a superb cast and a lavish technical setting, it would have been a hit anyway. But it also had unforgettable tunes, like "Somewhere over the Rainbow . . . and "If I only had a brain, a heart, the nerve", written especially for the movie, rather than adapted from old songs.

[151]

POPULAR MUSIC continued its march to greater technical competence throughout the 1930's. What Gershwin, Kern and Porter had started in the decade before, alert newcomers to Tin Pan Alley carried to further heights. Sophisticated swing replaced crude jazz; new stars vied with old timers in the radio spotlight; record companies had all but failed as the phonograph was retired to the attic.

The battle of the airways was gargantian. Rival broadcasting chains, each aware that songs and singers were what put their programs across, pirated talent and drove salaries to heights that even the dizzy amusement world considered dizzying. Some radio stars bought into the music concerns that published the songs they plugged. In spite of general indifference to making one's own music and the increasing complexities of popular song, there was still quite a bit of business built around song sheet sales. Even though one could not hit all the high notes, it was still possible to hum around the tune, or play simplified versions on whatever instrument one could command. And towards the end of the decade, when the novelty of radio was wearing thin and long familiarity with radio songsters was beginning to breed indifference, a new trend began to assert itself. Cowboy songs and hillbilly music made their appearance. First aired over local stations rather than national networks, the very simplicity of such music began to win out with an ear surfieted by technically adroit songs. The hillbillys were more like what everyone could sing. Without being aware of why, the public had begun to turn away from such high-tone popular classics as *Smoke Gets In Your Eyes* and to call for *The Last Roundup*. Also, they were looking for a way of having such tunes made easily available whenever they wanted to play them.

1940

Juke Box Jamboree . . .

THE COMEBACK of the phonograph record was nothing short of phenomenal. All but forgotten during the public's fascination with radio, it staged a terrific return. This was due to a combination of reasons. But mainly radio listening was now "old Hat." People were looking for a new and different way to enjoy music. They found it in the automatic record machines that had begun to appear in bars, soda fountains and eateries of all sorts,—in fact, everywhere groups congregated. One could drop a nickel in the slot, select the orchestra or song of his choice, then hum or dance to the music produced. Young folks staged impromptu parties around these automatic music makers. Old Folks liked them too. It was the era of JUKE BOX JAMBOREE.

Canned-music had grown like a green bay tree since its early 20th Century start; not until the advent of radio had it seemed anything like a healthy young giant. But those who thought that the awful slump in sales in the '30s meant the end had reckoned without the ingenuity of the phonograph makers. With electrical pickups, mechanical changers and cheap, electrically transcribed records of popular bands and singers, the phonograph business had modernized itself and grown bigger than ever. By 1948 there were 775 companies, big and small, making records which sold for around $300,000,000 a year. And that was only the beginning of the product's earning power! Over half a million glittering juke-boxes were in operation throughout the land, each of which took in around $30.00 a week. The nation's radio stations also played records, usually as part of an advertising program. A new profession, that of Disc Jockey, had developed.

Naturally, all this emphasis on canned music had resulted in technological unemployment for many musicians. In 1942 all union musicians quit from recording studios until a royalty was paid on sales of every record made. The union got what it wanted. For the public demanded of broadcasters and record makers that their favorite songs and bands be made available to them at any and all times. In fact, so prevalent was the public airing of canned music one could not escape it during the day's work, even if he wished.

RUSTIC RHYTHM REAPS REWARD. In the late 1940's the trend
that started a decade before had assumed landslide proportions. We
refer, of course, to the establishment of hillbilly music as a major
segment of the amusement industry. Several things may account for
this rise. One was the popularity of hill-billy bands and a revival of
interest in country dances. Another was the hold which low cost
talent (It don't take much to sing hill-billy) attained on radio audiences
when broadcast over local stations. Still another was the development
of a new type "horse opera" by the movies. Born of a desire to cut
expenses, the usual drama of ride and shoot was now interspersed
with "western ranch music" played by bands like the one Paramount
dressed above or sung by such singing cowboys as Gene Autry and
Roy Rogers. In a country-wide survey, *Billboard* magazine discovered
almost 100 folk-music parks giving shows with local or imported
hill-billy talent at least once a week. Spreading westward from the
east, these parks featured a huge outdoor stage and had an average
attendance of 4,000 people, it was reported.

Individual hill-billy songs maintained their hold on public fancy
about two months, were literally dinned to death by incessant radio and
juke box plugging. Who can remember tunes of songs on opposite page.

[156]

IN THE LATE 40's novelty dance bands like that above had become
the rage of many nightclubs. At Chicago's Blackhawk, band leader-
song writer Al Trace was packing in the customers with a variety of
corn straight off the cob. His band would occasionally play sweet
music for dancing, but featured 'hick' numbers like *You Call Everybody
Darling* and *Brush Those Tears From Your Eyes*. Trace developed his
songs while writing running material for WLS National Barn Dance.
Another top clownster was Red Ingle, a band leader whose off-the-cuff
parody on *Nature Boy* sold around a million records. The piece began
with a wolf call and ended with all the instruments thrown into a
corner. It's words were, "A boy I mean was oh so peachy keen, a
real gone guy from Goneville," and it was scored for "ukelele, kazoo,
'hogan twanger' (wooden box strung with hacksaw blades) and
Indian elephant bell."

The credo of these latter day song writers was well expressed by
Jules Styne (*Give Me Five Minutes More*) "We make our songs easy
to memember and easy to sing; songs the guy in the locker room and
the woman in the farmhouse can sing without a piano. . Give 'em what
they understand. . don't try to elevate them. You gotta write for the
people. Art is great, sure; but who can sing Shostakovich?"

[157]

NEW HORIZONS in the popular music field were set when song pluggers like Frank Sinatra and Jo Stafford scored hits with hillbilly versions of *That's How Much I Love You Baby* and *Temptation*. Even Bing Crosby began to sing westerns. Songs like the titles above rocketed from obscurity to become best sellers. Record makers who had once laughed at "singing cowboys", were not caught napping long. Here are some more titles (the tunes all tend to sound alike) that have enjoyed wide acceptance in the juke box trade: *I'll Dance At Your Wedding; Deep In The Heart Of Texas; You Call Everybody Darling; I Tipped My Hat And Slowly Rode Away; Hair Of Gold, Eyes Of Blue; Jingle, Jangle, Jingle; Candy Kisses; Jealous Heart; Life Gets Tejus.*

THE NOVELTY SONG. Folks who had cut their teeth on the songs of Kern and Gershwin said that popular music was deteriorating. Perhaps not as technically adroit as those of the 20's, some of the later songs had a subtle appeal all their own. The five pictured above will be long remembered as "clever", to say the least. So will such other novelty numbers as *Chatanooga Choo Choo; Tico Tico; Zip-A-Dee-Do-Da; Doing What Comes Naturally; On The Atchison, Topeka And The Sante Fe; Don't Sit Under The Apple Tree; Baby It's Cold Outside* and *It's Love, Love, Love.* One great novelty number, (*Hut Sut Song*), was once (1941) banned as a public nuisance; but its composer went right on to such popular hits as *I Dood It; How Soon* and *Hi Neighbor.*

JUST AS DOPESTERS had it all figured out that radio had killed the phonograph forever, along came the automatic record changer to give it new life. Of the battles between rival recording concerns and their products this account can have little to say. It is sufficient to mention that at one time three major companies presented to a bewildered public three different recording and playing systems, records that ran at one of three different speeds. Naturally, one had to have the right player for the right record and vice versa. Order and agreement finally prevailed, with all recording moving towards the more economical, long-playing, slow-turning records.

Above and on the right are sample advertising pages from the late 1940's that accurately reflect the public's musical mood. Fran Warren and Perry Como were relative newcomers among reigning favorites. Dance bands had begun to turn backwards to record the great songs of great composers throughout the half-century. The curious fact about popular music is that kids in 1949 were likely to be dancing to the same tunes as did their mothers and fathers back in 1920's and the 1930's. A glance at some of the song titles listed on the opposite page is convincing evidence. Look up their dates of original publication in the back of the book.

90 all-time hits!

"TEX BENEKE plays HOAGY CARMICHAEL"

Star Dust, Lazy River, Lazy Bones, Rockin' Chair, Georgia on My Mind, Riverboat Shuffle.

SPADE COOLEY plays BILLY HILL"

The Last Round-Up, Wagon Wheels, Lights Out, In the Chapel in the Moonlight, Empty Saddles, The Old Spinning Wheel.

TOMMY DORSEY plays COLE PORTER"

Just One of Those Things, Love for Sale, Why Shouldn't I, You Do Something to Me, I Get a Kick Out of You, It's Delovely.

RALPH FLANAGAN plays RODGERS & HAMMERSTEIN"

Some Enchanted Evening, People Will Say We're In Love, The Surrey With the Fringe on Top, It Might as Well Be Spring, If I Loved You; Oh, What a Beautiful Mornin'.

"LARRY GREEN plays VINCENT YOUMANS"

Tea for Two, Carioca, Time On My Hands, More Than You Know, Sometimes I'm Happy, I Want To Be Happy.

"ERSKINE HAWKINS plays W. C. HANDY"

St. Louis Blues, Careless Love, Memphis Blues, Aunt Hagar's Children, Beale Street Blues, John Henry Blues.

"SPIKE JONES plays THE CHARLESTON"

The Charleston, Charlestono-Mio, Black Bottom, Doin' the New Raccoon, I Wonder Where My Baby Is Tonight, Varsity Drag.

"SAMMY KAYE plays IRVING BERLIN"

Blue Skies, Always, How Deep Is the Ocean, Say It Isn't So, A Pretty Girl Is Like a Melody, Alexander's Ragtime Band.

"WAYNE KING plays JOHANN STRAUSS"

The Blue Danube; Wine, Women and Song; Tales From the Vienna Woods, Emperor Waltz, You and You, Voices of Spring.

"FREDDY MARTIN plays JEROME KERN"

Make Believe, All the Things You Are, Smoke Gets In Your Eyes, I've Told Every Little Star, The Song Is You, Who.

"RAY McKINLEY plays RODGERS AND HART"

My Heart Stood Still, Blue Moon, You Took Advantage of Me, It's Easy To Remember, Blue Room, Thou Swell.

"VAUGHN MONROE plays VICTOR HERBERT"

Ah! Sweet Mystery of Life, Toyland, Kiss Me Again, Indian Summer, Gypsy Love Song, I'm Falling In Love With Someone.

"CLAUDE THORNHILL plays GEORGE GERSHWIN"

Oh, Lady, Be Good; Bidin' My Time, The Man I Love, Summertime, Embraceable You, Fascinatin' Rhythm.

"MIGUELITO VALDES plays ERNESTO LECUONA"

The Breeze and I, La Comparsa, Malaguena, Say Si Si, Always in My Heart, Jungle Drums.

"CHARLIE VENTURA plays DUKE ELLINGTON"

It Don't Mean a Thing, Sophisticated Lady, Solitude, Take the "A" Train, Mood Indigo, Prelude to a Kiss.

RCA

The Billboard
JUKE BOX SUPPLEMENT

EVERY MUSIC

OPERATOR KNOWS...

get the play!

Juke Box Standard Favorites

In a poll conducted last fall among several hundred juke box operators recordings of the following standards were voted by the operators as the standard tunes which have made most money for operators down thru the years.

RATING	SONG TITLE
1	Star Dust
2	Begin the Beguine
3	Blue Skies
4	On the Sunny Side of the Street
5	Always
6	Night and Day
7	Temptation
8	Easter Parade
9	Beer Barrel Polka
10	Alexander's Ragtime Band
11	April Showers
12	My Blue Heaven
13	Smoke Gets in Your Eyes
14	Body and Soul
15	Embraceable You
16	I Can't Give You Anything But Love, Baby
17	Tea for Two
18	Dancing in the Dark
19	Tico Tico
20	All the Things You Are

BILLBOARD MAGAZINE kept tract of songs that were juke box hits throughout the 1940's. Their list, divided according to "Race, folk and pop," does not jibe with popularity counts based on radio, movie and stage presentations. But it is probably a more accurate estimate of what the average teenster liked and would put a nickel in the slot to hear. The leading 25 numbers are listed above.

[162]

GREAT GOD JUKE. Take a tip from these record ads and salaam before his majesty! Whether you're away on vacation or out for an evening in your own home town, be sure to get your refreshments where you can put a nickel in the slot and choose a tuneful accompaniment to sipping. Sweet or swing, jazz or jive, rollicking polka or hill-billy ballad, Perry Como or Vaughn Monroe, Russ Morgan or Spike Jones, they are all there and anxious to please you. You are bowing before a multi-million-dollar industry!

HEY! BA-BA-RE-BOP

By LIONEL HAMPTON · CURLEY HAMNER

As Recorded by
LIONEL HAMPTON
On Decca

featured by
LIONEL HAMPTON
and his Orchestra

SOME THINK that the lyric of a song leads in importance, the melody second and the rhythm of the melody not at all. Be-bop experts, however, say it's the rhythm behind the melody, the emotion that it dredges up, which carrys today's song in popular appeal.

[164]

POST WAR DANCE MUSIC moved in two seemingly contrary directions. Led by the *avant guarde* of jazz, jitterbugs swung and stomped their way through innumerable examples of swing, boogie woogie and be-bop. But those who turned their backs on such carryings on were caught up in revivals of the hardly less energetic polkas and square dances. Actually, both the jitterbugger and the revivalist were seeking a more carefree, less inhibited form of dance expression. Frustrations of post-war world and its uneasy peace found outlet in roisterous movement. Above are five polkas that found favor with music makers. Country dances attracted city slickers from miles around.

CONTENDER to Kern and Hammerstein's *Show Boat* (1927) for top musical comedy honors if Rodgers and Hammerstein's *Oklahoma* (1943). As native as American Corn, it tells simple story.

1. Curley Wins Laurey at basket lunch. Everyone has come dressed in Sunday best to square-dance.

2. Jud, the hired man, lusts for Laurey. His pictures of Can-Can dancers provide occasion for ballet.

3. But Curley arrives to rescue Laurey from her bad dreams of Jud, makes her his bride.

4. And in final scene, the pair start on their honeymoon, singing *Surrey with the Fringe on the Top*

WITH RECORD RUN of 2,246 performances on Broadway alone, *Oklahoma* music was closely integrated with story and dancing.

SONGS FROM these great musicals have found their way to America's heart. All three were produced by Rodgers and Hammerstein. *Carosel* is preferred by some to *Oklahoma*; and South Pacific—starring Mary Martin and Erico Pinza—broke the records of both earlier shows. Hammerstein lyrics are so right in every sense for Rogers music that one can almost hear the tune the moment he begins to read the words. Take "chicks–and ducks–and geese–better scurry; when–I take–you out–in the surrey; when I take you out in the surrey–with the fringe on top." One of the loveliest songs in Oklahoma, *Surrey*, starts briskly, gradually slows towards the end, simulating pace of actual ride. Jud's song "The floor creaks, the door squeaks, a field mouse a nibblin' on the broom" helps set perfect mood for "by myself in a lonely room." Hammerstein's collaborations with several great composers raises the mute question as to what their songs would have been without his lyrics. Hammerstein has fashioned so many rhythms that are familiar to so many people that he is rightly called the number one lyricist of Tin Pan Alley. With 30 musicals and 1000 songs to his credit, he holds the coveted AA rating by ASCAP, is estimated to collect a cool half-million yearly in royalties. Sometimes compared to Sir William Gilbert, he is really in a class all by himself.

[168]

WITHIN 24 HOURS after Pearl Harbor, Tin Pan Alley tunesters had "quickies" like *Ax The Axis* readied for sale. Best of early war songs paid their respects to the Air Force, included *Keep 'Em Flying, He Wears A Pair Of Silver Wings* and the official Army Air Corps' *Off We Go Into The Wild Blue Yonder*. Older branches of the service already had their official songs though *Bell Bottom Trousers* quickly became unofficial in the Navy. *Praise The Lord And Pass The Ammunition* is a song built around a chance remark of a fighting chaplain. Other war songs included *He's 1A In The Army and He's A1 In My Heart, Blue Birds Over The White Cliffs Of Dover, Remember Pearl Harbor* and *Coming In On A Wing And A Prayer*. Radio singers like Kate Smith and Vaughn Monroe did their bit to raise morale by singing *Any Bonds Today, Arms For The Love Of America, America, I Love You, We Did It Before* and *God Bless America*. But there was little singing by the troops themselves. Possibly this was because the mechanicals (radio, movies and phonographs) had bred a race of spectators rather than participants in song. Elaborate programs were instituted to bring stars like Bob Hope and Dinah Shore overseas to entertain the boys. Who will ever forget the gay performance of *Hey, Good Lookin'* or the heart-touching *He's A Right Guy*.

WORLD WAR II did not produce songs of the calibre of *Tipperary* and *Over There* nor did soldiers go off to war singing blithely as before. Disillusionment was upon them before they started. For the first time songs like the above appeared.

[170]

POWDER YOUR FACE WITH SUNSHINE

SMILE! SMILE! SMILE!

Words and Music by CARMEN LOMBARDO and STANLEY ROCHINSKI

1948

LEBERT

CARMEN

Featured by
GUY LOMBARDO
and his Royal Canadians

Lombardo
MUSIC, Inc.
1619 BROADWAY NEW YORK 19 N Y

GREATEST, and almost only, smiles song to come out of World War II, was this lilting number, originally from the pen of a hospitalized war veteran.

[171]

BROADWAY MUSICAL SHOWS were again plentiful in the 1940's, of which those represented by the Playbills above are typical. Gay and giddy, paced with fast chatter, they produced few memorable songs. Al Jolson's last show (Hold On To Your Hats) quickly closed. Bobby Clark was a bit more successful. Irving Berlin's *Louisiana Purchase* brought Victor Moore and Irene Bordini back to Broadway but made no lasting impression. *Lend An Ear* poked fun at old time musicals of the 1920's, prepared the way for Carol Channing's later nostalgic hit *Gentlemen Prefer Blonds*. None of the shows quite had the vitality, that make *Something For The Boys* a memorable occasion.

SOMETHING FOR THE BOYS, compounded from Cole Porter's words and music, and delivered by Ethel Merman. Besides this rollicking score, Cole Porter had another 1940's "great," *Kiss Me Kate.*

SOUVENIR BOOKLET from the show indicates type of songs and performers who made it a hit. Show-topper—Irving Berlin, dressed in World War I uniform and singing *I Hate To Get Up In The Morning*!

[174]

HIGH SPOT of World War II songs and musical shows was provided by the show Irving Berlin wrote, produced and took on the road to boost morale and to provide Army Emergency Relief funds.

BETTY GRABLE was No. 1 pin up girl of World War II, sang and danced G.I. Joe many a morale-building tune. In the chaos of post-war Hollywood, Grable musical was about only sure fire "box-office" left.

MOVIE SONG HITS. Though by this time many a Tin Pan Alley tunesmith had beaten a path back to Gotham, enough were left in Hollywood to keep the sound tract well supplied. Rarely was the show as tuneful as Rodgers and Hammerstein's *State Fair*. Rarely indeed did it produce a bouncy number like *Buttons and Bows* that caught on in the hinterland long before the picture itself could be released. More frequently, it was not the song, but the personality of a star, like Betty Grable, that put the numbers across. The like of Betty had never been seen before or since. By own admission, she was not a great singer or dancer. Yet to her public, she could do no wrong.

[177]

THE GIRL THAT I MARRY

IN THE LATE 1940's, as in a decade before, irrepressible Ethel Merman was still 'wowing' them with numbers like, *Doing What Comes Naturally*. Few stars had her enormous vitality, could so completely capture a role. To most, Merman will always be *Annie Get Your Gun*.

[178]

JUKE BOXES held sway throughout the 1940's. Their pull with the public was never seriously challenged during the decade. Only the 1950's, with their emphasis on television, halted the tide. No wonder that record makers ran ads eulogizing the coin machine operators.

AS JUKE BOX and automatic record changer began to take over somewhat from Radio, song pluggers assumed even greater importance. Rival diskeries fought for the services of personalities who could put over a song. Above are some of the best—both tunes and tunesters: The Mills Brothers, that fabulous foursome who, with one guitar for a background, made their voices blend to sound like a jazz orchestra; Dinah Shore, voted No. 1 favorite again and again by disc jockeys; Margaret Whiting, singing daughter of composer R. E. Whiting; the Andrews Sisters; Frank Sinatra. In the year 1941 one hundred eleven *million* records were sold in the U. S. alone. The output grew.

THE STRAIGHT NUMBER still had its following, as indicated by the song covers above. Conspicuously absent in this array is *Nature Boy*, hit tune written by an almost unbelievable character who signed himself eden ahbez ("Only God and the Infinite should be capitalized"). An Indian Yogi by way of Kansas and Brooklyn, he wore a beard and long hair, practiced breath control, slept outdoors, ate only fruits and nuts. Reporters found him "cute" or "queer" but neither of these adjectives could be rightly applied to the song which went "there was a boy. . a very strange enchanted boy." *There* the verdict was "hot stuff." In explaining himself, Eden said, "In my body I am of the West, In my soul, I am of the East, in my music I am both.

THE SWING of popular fancy towards so-called 'hill-billy music' represented a dominant trend throughout the 1940's. Various factors contributed to this shift. As juke boxes and radio-phonographs enlarged their outlets by postwar expansion, it became possible to get more accurate checks on the real popularity of a song than ever before. No longer were tastes set by a relatively small group of Broadway and Hollywood showmen. Through juke box returns and record sales, a general public widely dispersed in the hinterlands had shown an unmistakable preference for simple melodies and rustic rhythms. Even city dwellers raised on Gershwin and Kern were attracted by the jingle-jangle of hill-billy music. Possibly a large section of the public had been surfieted on the beautiful but involved tunes of the last twenty years. Possibly it was the very great availability of cheap talent that helped vault this new folk-music into popuarlity. But whatever the causes, the *fact* was crystal clear. In the 1940's popular song began to turn away from the elaborate musicianship which had developed steadily throughout the half century here reviewed; it was turning away from sophistication in both tune and verse and moving back towards an expression of simple folk music. For many observers, this shift seemed all to the good. Though they might not care for much of the untutorea hill-billy music currently recorded and broadcast, they felt that its popularity would encourage even the best song writers to reach back to grass roots. And with the revival of interest in folk music and folk dancing, perhaps our popular songs would become once more music of the people, sung by all the people.

1950

Continued Performance

WE HAVE COME TO the half-century mark. It's time to take a long look backwards—back through the songs already recalled, back over the means taken to popularize them. Is there any single tie between the era of Close Harmony and the era of Juke Box Jamboree? Do 1910's Piano Accompaniment, 1920's Phonograph Fever and 1930's Music In The Air play any common chords? Is there, in short, anything like a CONTINUED PERFORMANCE?

Certainly no communality of song style, no common manner of rendition holds the decades together. Various singers, various instruments have risen and fallen in popularity. The average person has shifted from making his own music to being a listener. Popular songs have themselves grown increasingly technical, more adroitly phrased, more richly orchestrated. Only in subject matter have they remained virtually unchanged. Barring purely topical numbers, the song subjects that interested people in 1900 still interest them today. Here alone is there record of Continued Performance.

What are the subjects that people like to sing about or to have sung to them? *Mother*, for one; *Home*, for another; *America*, for another. But over and above all these is the greatest subject of all—*Love*. Without attempting to make any accurate count, we may estimate that over three-fourths of the popular songs of the last fifty years have dealt, directly or indirectly, with Boy Meets Girl. Look back through the songs recalled on these pages and note the ones that are still as popular as the day they were written. Almost invariably they are love songs!

That Americans still sing of love is readily understandable. Living in a civilization that surrounds sex expression with many taboos and restraints, our popular songs have long served as safety valves and substitute satisfactions. By accepted convention, many things can be said in song that would be considered bad taste, smutty or oversentimental when directly expressed, even in a novel. Singing "I love you" to a girl does not constitute a proposal of marriage; nor does a bawdy ballad mark the locker-room quartet as unprincipled rakes!

[185]

Whether honestly sentimental or downright suggestive, our love songs fill a very vital niche in the American Way of Life. That is why *Dear Old Girl* and *Sweet Adeline* continue to exist as popular favorites along with the latest hill-billy expressions of this same theme. Sigmund Spaeth, the top musical pundit of our day, has commented many times on the indestructible character of the love lyric. In one place (*The Facts of Life in Popular Song*, New York, McGraw-Hill, 1934) he writes as follows: "To a large percentage of the population the popular song also supplies a convenient substitute for conversation. Things that the soda clerk would not dare say to the shop girl, even if he commanded the necessary English, ripple from his lips quite nonchalantly from the hit of the moment, particularly if accompanied by its music. All the techniques of flirtation, as well as the more serious declarations of affection or suggestions of intimacy, find a handy textbook in the literature of popular song. Often the protagonists themselves are scarcely aware of what they are saying, but generally they have an inkling. At least it sounds like something very smart and snappy. It is all a part of our fast-working, well routined machine age, dealing in formulas, in slogans, in short cuts, but often side-stepping honest realities."

Love, then, sacred or profane, is the most universally popular subject of song. But this does not mean that styles in treating the subject have remained unchanged throughout the half-century. Quite the contrary is true. Take 1890's *After the Ball* and *Oh, Promise Me* as a start and compare them with 1950's *Cuddle Buggin Baby* and *I'm Playing With Fire;* the sentiment might be the same, but certainly not its vocal expression. We have moved a long ways from the high-faluting style that produced "Gentle Zebella, banish they fear, Love's retornell, tarry and hear." Early 20th century song sometimes drew elaborate artificial parallels to the love life of the birds and the bees in getting its human message across. "*Oh, Had I Wings Like A Dove*" was a favored way of saying it. But with general acceptance of the "coon song" and ragtime, the bewitchment of girl for boy could take the form of "*I'd leave ma happy home for you.*" One could get off pretty risque comments in *My gal's a high born lady*. Soon even Caucasians were making imaginary whoopee to Von Tilzer's "*Under the Yum-Yum Tree.*"

By the middle of the century, popular songs made it increasingly clear that the female of the species was not a saint or goddess or disembodied spirit, but an exciting flesh and blood creature under her clothes. Flirtation began to get its rightful consideration in social intercourse and its technical details were aired with increasing boldness in the love songs of the day. *Kissing on the Sly* led up to Victor Herbert's *Kiss Me Again* and his *Kiss in the Dark*. The earlier vogue of giving a girl's name to a song (*Daisy Bell, on a bicycle built for two*) was revived in *Margie*. In keeping with the jazz tempo of the age, song events moved rapidly (*Me and the boy friend, the boy friend and me, we stick together like sap on a tree*) and overtly suggestive lines widely accepted.

But there was whimsicality and honest sentiment, too, in many of these quarter century numbers; "*I took one look at you, that's all I meant to do, and then my heart stood still.*" It is a mistake to think of all the popular songs of the 20's and 30's as vulgar and jazzy. Look at *Just Mollie and me, and baby makes three, we're happy in my blue heaven.* Certainly this has just as many earmarks of respectable domesticity as *I want a girl, just like the girl that married dear old dad.* True, if one is looking for it, he can find a great deal of salacious material in latter-day love songs. With "It" standing for sex appeal in general and "Thing" a phallic symbol, song writers have produced such numbers as *Let's do it again, You've got that thing* and *Wouldja for a big red apple.* Then there are the "beautifully sexy" songs like *Why can't this night go on forever, Body and Soul* and *As you desire me.* Those who are tempted to link this all up with flaming youth might well question if the effect of these songs was any more torrid than today's rowdy hill-billy ballads. It is yet an unproved proposition that the loosening of verbal restraints in popular song has also been accompanied by a loosening in morals. One might indeed argue quite the opposite way, argue that as the facts of life are sung out in the open, gayly and cleanly, there is much less *sotto-voce* lovemaking.

Always running side-by-side with love songs of levity and lightness are those of polite melancholy. *Come to me my melancholy baby* and *Roomful of Roses* are early and late versions dealing with the ache of true love. Which type does the public like the best? It would be difficult to say. We do know, however, that the greatest sales records and most enduring memories stem from heart songs. Everyone has his favorite list of such songs. None would surely agree in all particulars. But it is certain that these five songs will be on most lists: From the 1900 period we have chosen *Sweet Adeline*; from the 1910's *I Want a Girl*; from the 1920's, *Tea for Two;* from the 1930's, *Goodnight Sweetheart;* and from the 1940's, *People Will Say We're in Love.* Such songs represent a cross-section of honest sentimentality, have always been far better sellers than any tricky, overwrought, wisecracking, musical aphrodisiacs that have yet been devised. They constitute, in fact, a golden restatement of the eternal proposition that *It's love for aye.*

TIMES MAY CHANGE and fashions in verse, but love goes on forever. Old and young, today and yesterday, they all sing of love.
Whether it is called *You are My Lucky Star* or *That's For Me* makes

[188]

little difference. In every day and every way, through comedy or tragedy, by ribald suggestiveness or mysterious allusion, everyone is interested in songs that treat of heart's desire. These alone endure.

We have reached the end of our story and some self-styled authorities will say that the hey-day of popular song writing is past. That is doubtful. But if we look at what is going on in music today, one conclusion is inescapable. Fully as much interest is accorded old songs as is given to new ones. The curious fact about popular music is that kids going to their first important dances in 1950 are likely to dance to the same tunes as did their mothers and fathers back in the 1920's and 1930's. Today's bobby-soxers may have found new idols in Perry Como and Billy Eckstine, but they croon the same songs that helped make Rudy Vallee, Bing Crosby and Frank Sinatra household names. Juke-box melodies provide today's teensters with the same theme music as helped out the old-folks when they were young and in love. Consider just one bygone year as an example. The ancients of 1930 were the first to sing, dance and listen to such tunes as *Beyond the Blue Horizon, Body and Soul, Cheerful Little Earful, Dancing with Tears in My Eyes, Embraceable You, I Got Rhythm, Little White Lies, The Stein Song, Sunny Side of the Street, Three Little Words, Time on My Hands, Two Hearts in Three-quarter Time, What is this thing called Love, Walking my baby back home,* and *You're Driving me Crazy.* If this not enough to show the children why mother and dad know today's hits before they do, look at the song covers surrounding the picture of Irving Berlin!

Certainly, the most enduring popular songs are those that give expression to the art of love. The half-century mark has recently provided several authorities the occasion to list the ten best songs since the rise of Tin Pan Alley. The basis for such lists runs all the way from statistics on sheet music sales and royalties earned to public opinion polls and personal preference. Sigmund Spaeth concentrates on the songs of the first two decades; a well-known music publisher prefers those of the 1920's; a band leader measures everything by *Stardust;* a song leader says that most recent songs are unsingable, lists only those favored by community sings. But while the individual songs chosen differ from list to list, it is interesting to find that at least three-quarters of them are always love songs; one list, in fact, has nothing but this type of number!

Appreciation is long overdue for those song writers whose influence on their times—in love affairs aided, joys and sorrows given expression, and so on—makes even presidents seem minor figures. The number of enduring songs that men like Berlin have helped put into the nations noggin is nothing short of remarkable. In Berlin's case alone, they number into the hundreds. His *Alexander's Ragtime Band* is still in the forefront of popularity with ten big name bands recently making recordings of it. In 1912 he commemorated the death of his

first wife with the beautiful *When I lost you;* In 1914 it was *I want to go back to Michigan,* recently referred to as *Down on the Farm* and plugged by the Andrews sisters; Al Jolson sings the 1917 hit, *Someone else may be there when I'm gone,* and everyone has heard, and sung, *God Bless America.* In 1919 Berlin wrote *A Pretty Girl is like a Melody;* in 1920 it was *Tell Me Little Gipsy;* in 1921 *Say it with Music;* 1922 gave us *Crinoline Days* among many others; 1924, *All Alone* and *What'll I Do;* in 1925 it was *Always* and *Remember;* in 1926, *How Many Times.* Coming into the 1930's, we find (Jolson's favorite) *Let Me Sing and I'll be Happy* and *Say it Isn't So;* then there is *Easter Parade* (1933), *Cheek to Cheek* (1935), and *I've Got my Love to Keep me Warm* (1937).

Unlike most song writers, Berlin was the exception that seemed to get better the older he grew. In just one year (1942) he put out the following enduring favorites: *This is the Army, Mr. Jones, I'm getting Tired, I left My Heart at The Stage Door Canteen,* and the song which more than any other Irving Berlin melody is surely marching down into our folk music, *White Christmas.* No other song writer, unless it be Stephan Foster, has been so prolific, has had so many sure-fire hits, so many firsts in song innovation. Partly his success seems to rest with the fact that, like Foster, he writes both the words and music. They belong together like bread and butter. Hail to Berlin and all the other song writers who have left their impress on the times! [191]

SONG AND DANCE STYLES often move in cycles. 1950 has already seen a revival of the Charleston and its associated dance tunes. A glance at the period covers above should show Today's youngsters why their parents often know their song hits before they do.

50 Years of Song Hits...

This list of song hits for the last 50 years has been compiled for the convenience of persons interested in recalling the songs that all America sang during any particular year. Basis for inclusion is mainly in terms of sheet music sales and/or performance royalties.

Phonograph records are available for a great number of these songs. Consult Jack Burton, *Blue Book of Tin Pan Alley* (Century House, 1950) for exact catalogue number of each recording.

Credit for listing current copyright holders is due *Billboard* magazine and *The American Society of Composers, Authors and Publishers* (ASCAP) and *Broadcast Music, Inc.* (BMI).

1900
(ASCAP)

Bird in a Gilded Cage, A
Harry Von Tilzer Music Pub. Co.
Goodbye Dolly Gray
Shapiro, Bernstein & Co., Inc.
I Can't Tell Why I Love You, But I Do
Paull-Pioneer Music Corp.
Ma Blushin' Rose
M. Witmark & Sons
Strike Up the Band—Here Comes a Sailor
Harry Von Tilzer Music Pub. Co.
Tell Me Pretty Maiden
Edwin H. Morris & Co., Inc.

(BMI)

Down South
Marks
Old Flag Never Touched the Ground
Marks

1901
(ASCAP)

Blaze Away
Leo Feist, Inc.
Hiawatha
Remick Music Corp.
I Love You Truly
Carrie Jacobs-Bond & Son

Just A'wearying for You
Carrie Jacobs-Bond & Son
Mighty Lak' a Rose
John Church Co.
O Dry Those Tears
Chappell & Co., Inc.

(BMI)

My Castle on the Nile
Marks
Maiden With the Dreamy Eyes
Marks

1902
(ASCAP)

Because (d'Hardelot)
Chappell & Co., Inc.
Down Where the Wurtzburger Flows
Harry Von Tilzer Music Pub. Co.
In the Sweet Bye and Bye
Harry Von Tilzer Music Pub. Co.
On a Sunday Afternoon
Harry Von Tilzer Music Pub. Co.
Please Go 'Way and Let Me Sleep
Harry Von Tilzer Music Pub. Co.

(BMI)

Glow Worm
Marks

In the Good Old Summertime
Marks
Oh, Didn't He Ramble
Marks
Under the Bamboo Tree
Marks

1903
(ASCAP)
Bedelia
Remick Music Corp.
Dear Old Girl
Leo Feist, Inc.
Four Indian Love Lyrics
(*1*) *The Temple Bells*
(*2*) *Less Than the Dust*
(*3*) *Kashmiri Song*
(*4*) *Till I Wake*
Boosey & Co., Ltd.
The March of the Toys
M. Witmark & Sons
Sweet Adeline
T. B. Harms Co.
Toyland
M. Witmark & Sons

(BMI)
Congo Love Song
Marks
Ida, Sweet as Apple Cider
Marks
Lazy Moon
Marks
Where the Sunset Turns the Ocean's Blue to Gold
Marks

1904
(ASCAP)
Give My Regards to Broadway
Jerry Vogel Music Co., Inc.
Goodbye Little Girl Goodbye
M. Witmark & Sons
Goodbye, My Lady Love
Mills Music, Inc.
Teasing
G. Schirmer, Inc.
The Yankee Doodle Boy
Jerry Vogel Music Co., Inc.

(BMI)
Come Take a Trip in My Airship
Marks

1905
(ASCAP)
Forty-Five Minutes From Broadway
Jerry Vogel Music Co., Inc.
I Want What I Want When I Want It
M. Witmark & Sons

194

In My Merry Oldsmobile
M. Witmark & Sons
In the Shade of the Old Apple Tree
Remick Music Corp.
Kiss Me Again (*If I Was on the Stage*)
M. Witmark & Sons
Mary's a Grand Old Name
Jerry Vogel Music Co., Inc.
My Gal Sal
Edward B. Marks Corp.
Rufus Rastus Johnson Brown
Harry Von Tilzer Music Pub. Co.
So Long Mary
Jerry Vogel Music Co., Inc.
Tammany
M. Witmark & Sons
Wait 'Til the Sun Shines, Nellie
Harry Von Tilzer Music Pub. Co.
Will You Love Me in December as You Do in May?
M. Witmark & Sons

(BMI)
Dearie
Marks
My Gal Sal
Marks
Nobody
Marks
When the Bell in the Lighthouse Rings
Marks

1906
(ASCAP)
At Dawning
Carl Fischer, Inc.
Because You're You
M. Witmark & Sons
He Walked Right In and Right Out Again
Fred Fischer Music Co., Inc.
I Just Can't Make My Eyes Behave
Shapiro, Bernstein & Co., Inc.
A Lemon in the Garden of Love
M. Witmark & Sons
Love Me and the World Is Mine
M. Witmark & Sons
Waiting at the Church or, My Wife Won't Let Me
Harms, Inc.
Waltz Me Around Again, Willie
Shapiro, Bernstein & Co., Inc.
What's the Use of Dreaming
Edward B. Marks Corp.
Won't You Come Over to My House
Remick Music Corp.
You're a Grand Old Flag
Jerry Vogel Music Co., Inc.

(BMI)
Bird on Nellie's Hat   Marks

1907
(ASCAP)

Because I'm Married Now
Shapiro, Bernstein & Co., Inc.
Budweiser's a Friend of Mine
Fred Fisher Music Co., Inc.
Down in the Old Cherry Orchard
Edward B. Marks Corp.
Harrigan
Jerry Vogel Music Co., Inc.
Honey Boy
Jerry Vogel Music Co., Inc.
I'm Tying the Leaves So They Won't Fall Down
Larry Spier, Inc.
On the Road to Mandalay
G. Schirmer, Inc.
School Days
Mills Music Inc.
Senora
Leo Feist, Inc.
Spring, Beautiful Spring
Edward B. Marks Corp.
Take Me Back to New York Town
Harry Von Tilzer Music Pub. Co.
There Never Was a Girl Like You
Remick Music Corp.

(BMI)

Hymns of the Old Church Choir   Marks
It's Delightful To Be Married   Marks

1908
(ASCAP)

Cuddle Up a Little Closer, Lovely Mine
Charles K. Harris
Daisies Won't Tell
Jerry Vogel Music Co., Inc.
Hoo-oo (Ain't You Coming Out Tonight)
Shapiro, Bernstein & Co., Inc.
Rainbow
Remick Music Corp.
Roses Bring Dreams of You
Shapiro, Bernstein & Co., Inc.
Smarty
Jerry Vogel Music Co., Inc.
Sunbonnet Sue
Shapiro, Bernstein & Co., Inc.
Take Me Out to the Ball Game
Jerry Vogel Music Co., Inc.
Yama Yama Man
M. Witmark & Sons
Yip-I-Addy-I-Ay
Shapiro, Bernstein & Co., Inc.

(BMI)

Be Sweet To Me, Kid
Marks

Honeymoon
Marks
If I Had a Thousand Lives To Live
Marks

1909
(ASCAP)

Blaze of Glory
Leo Feist, Inc.
Casey Jones
Shapiro, Bernstein & Co., Inc.
Cubanola Glide
Harry Von Tilzer Music Pub. Co.
Down Among the Sugar Cane
Mills Music, Inc.
Has Anybody Here Seen Kelly?
Famous Music Corp.
I Love My Wife, But Oh You Kid!
Jerry Vogel Music Co., Inc.
I've Got Rings on My Fingers
Harms, Inc.
I Wish I Had a Girl
Robbins Music Corp.
Meet Me Tonight in Dreamland
Shapiro, Bernstein & Co., Inc.
My Cousin Caruso
Remick Music Corp.
My Hero (from Chocolate Soldier).
M. Witmark & Sons
My Pony Boy
Jerry Vogel Music Co., Inc.
My Wife's Gone to the Country! Hurrah! Hurrah!
Irving Berlin, Inc.
Put on Your Old Grey Bonnet
Remick Music Corp.
Shine On Harvest Moon
Remick Music Corp.
When I Dream in the Gloaming of You
Shapiro, Bernstein & Co., Inc.

(BMI)

I Wonder Who's Kissing Her Now
Marks
I've Got a Pain in My Sawdust
Marks

1910
(ASCAP)

By the Light of the Silvery Moon
Remick Music Corp.
Ah! Sweet Mystery of Life
M. Witmark & Sons
All Aboard for Blanket Bay
Harry Von Tilzer Music Pub. Co.
All That I Ask of You Is Love
Shapiro, Bernstein & Co., Inc.
Alma, Where Do You Live?

195

Shapiro, Bernstein & Co., Inc.
Any Little Girl That's a Nice Little Girl
 Shapiro, Bernstein & Co., Inc.
A Perfect Day
 Carrie Jacobs-Bond & Son
Call Me Up Some Rainy Afternoon
 Irving Berlin, Inc.
Chinatown, My Chinatown
 Remick Music Corp.
Come Along My Mandy
 Jerry Vogel Music Co., Inc.
Come, Josephine, in My Flying Machine
 Shapiro, Bernstein & Co., Inc.
Day Dreams
 Edward B. Marks Corp.
Don't Wake Me Up, I'm Dreaming
 Shapiro, Bernstein & Co., Inc.
Down By the Old Mill Stream
 Forster Music Pub., Inc.
Every Beautiful Little Movement
 M. Witmark & Sons
Beautiful Garden of Roses
 Remick Music Corp.
I'm Falling in Love With Someone
 M. Witmark & Sons
Let Me Call You Sweetheart
 Shapiro, Bernstein & Co., Inc.
Mother Machree
 M. Witmark & Sons
On Mobile Bay
 Remick Music Corp.
Play That Barbershop Chord
 Shapiro, Bernstein & Co., Inc.
Put Your Arms Around Me Honey
 Broadway Music Corp.
Some of These Days
 Jerry Vogel Music Co., Inc.
Steamboat Bill
 Jerry Vogel Music Co., Inc.
Two Little Love Bees
 Edward B. Marks Corp.
You Are the Ideal of My Dreams
 Shapiro, Bernstein & Co., Inc.
What's the Matter With Father?
 Remick Music Corp.

1911

(ASCAP)

Alexander's Ragtime Band
 Irving Berlin, Inc.
All Alone (Von Tilzer)
 Harry Von Tilzer Music Pub. Co.
Everybody's Doin' It Now
 Irving Berlin, Inc.
Gaby Glide
 Shapiro, Bernstein & Co., Inc.

196

I Want a Girl, Just Like the Girl, etc.
 Harry Von Tilzer Music Pub. Co.
In the Shadows
 Edward B. Marks Corp.
My Beautiful Lady
 Chappell & Co., Inc.
My Lovin' Honey Man
 Leo Feist, Inc.
Oceana Roll
 Jerry Vogel Music Co., Inc.
Oh, You Beautiful Doll
 Remick Music Corp.
Somewhere a Voice Is Calling
 Harms, Inc.
That Mysterious Rag
 Irving Berlin, Inc.

1912

(ASCAP)

Be My Little Baby Bumble Bee
 Remick Music Corp.
Everybody Two Step
 Remick Music Corp.
Garland of Old Fashioned Roses
 O'Kay Music Co.
Giannina Mia (Friml)
 G. Schirmer, Inc.
Goodbye Rose
 Shapiro, Bernstein & Co., Inc.
In My Harem
 Irving Berlin, Inc.
Isle d'Amour
 Leo Feist, Inc.
It's a Long, Long Way to Tipperary
 B. Feldman & Co.-Chappell & Co., Inc.
Last Night Was the End of the World
 Harry Von Tilzer Music Pub. Co.
My Melancholy Baby
 Jerry Vogel Music Co., Inc.
On the Mississippi
 Shapiro, Bernstein & Co., Inc.
On Moonlight Bay
 Remick Music Corp.
Roll Dem Roly Boly Eyes
 Edward B. Marks Corp.
Row, Row, Row
 Harry Von Tilzer Music Pub. Co.
Sweetheart of Sigma Chi
 Melrose Bros.' Music Co., Inc.
That's How I Need You
 Leo Feist, Inc.
Waiting for the Robert E. Lee
 Southern
When I Get You Alone Tonight
 Leo Feist, Inc.
When I Lost You   Irving Berlin, Inc.

When Irish Eyes Are Smiling
  M. Witmark & Sons
When It's Apple Blossom Time in Normandy
  Remick Music Corp.
When the Midnight Choo-Choo Leaves for Alabam'
  Irving Berlin Music Co.

1913
(ASCAP)

Curse of an Aching Heart
  Leo Feist, Inc.
Don't Blame It All on Broadway
  Jerry Vogel Music Co., Inc.
Get Out and Get Under
  Irving Berlin, Inc.
Goodbye, Boys
  Harry Von Tilzer Music Pub. Co.
He'd Have To Get Under, Get Out and Get Under
  To Fix Up His Automobile
  Mills Music, Inc.
I Miss You Most of All
  Broadway Music Corp.
If I Had My Way
  Paull-Pioneer Music Corp.
Memphis Blues
  Handy Bros.' Music Co., Inc.
Nights of Gladness
  Edward B. Marks Corp.
On the Shores of Italy
  Leo Feist, Inc.
Peg O' My Heart
  Leo Feist, Inc.
Somebody Is Coming to My House
  Irving Berlin, Inc.
Sweethearts (Herbert)
  G. Schirmer, Inc.
There's a Girl in the Heart of Maryland
  Shapiro, Bernstein & Co., Inc.
Too-ra-loo-ra-loo-ral
  M. Witmark & Sons
Trail of the Lonesome Pine
  Shapiro, Bernstein & Co., Inc.
You Made Me Love You. I Didn't Want To Do It
  Broadway Music Corp.

(BMI)

El Choclo
  Marks

1914
(ASCAP)

By the Beautiful Sea
  Shapiro, Bernstein & Co., Inc.
Can't You Hear Me Calling, Caroline?
  M. Witmark & Sons
Goodbye Girls, I'm Through
  Chappell & Co., Inc.

He's a Devil in His Own Home Town
  Irving Berlin, Inc.
I Didn't Raise My Boy To Be a Soldier
  Leo Feist, Inc.
I Want To Go Back to Michigan, Down on the
  Farm
  Irving Berlin, Inc.
A Little Bit of Heaven
  Crawford Music Corp.
Missouri Waltz
  Forster Music Pub., Inc.
On the 5:15
  Remick Music Corp.
St. Louis Blues
  Handy Bros. Music Co., Inc.
Sylvia
  G. Schirmer, Inc.
There's a Little Spark of Love Still Burning
  Leo Feist, Inc.
They Didn't Believe Me (Kern)
  T. B. Harms Co.
This Is the Life
  Irving Berlin, Inc.
When You Play in the Game of Love
  Leo Feist, Inc.
When You're a Long, Long Way From Home
  Broadway Music Corp.
When You Wore a Tulip
  Leo Feist, Inc.
There's a Long, Long Trail
  M. Witmark & Sons

(BMI)

Ballin' the Jack
  Marks
Love's Own Sweet Song (Sari Waltz)   Marks

1915
(ASCAP)

Along the Rocky Road to Dublin
  Mills Music, Inc.
Auf Wiedersehen (Romberg)
  G. Schirmer, Inc.
Canadian Capers
  Remick Music Corp.
Down in Bom-Bombay
  Shapiro, Bernstein & Co., Inc.
Hello, Frisco
  M. Witmark & Sons
Hello, Hawaii, How Are You?
  Mills Music, Inc.
If We Can't Be the Same Old Sweethearts
  Leo Feist, Inc.
Just Try To Picture Me Down Home in Tennessee
  Mills Music Corp.
Keep the Home Fires Burning
  Chappell & Co., Inc.

197

Kiss Me Again (first time issued separately)
  Mlle. Modiste)
    M. Witmark & Sons
Memories
    Remick Music Corp.
M-O-T-H-E-R (*A Word That Means the World
  to Me*)
    Leo Feist, Inc.
My Mother's Rosary
    Mills Music Co.
*Pack Up Your Troubles in Your Old Kit Bag and
  Smile*
    Harms, Inc.
The Sunshine of Your Smile
    Harms, Inc.
The Little House Upon the Hill
    Shapiro, Bernstein & Co., Inc.
When I Leave the World Behind
    ABC Music Corp.

(BMI)

By Heck
    Marks
My Little Dream Girl
    Marks
My Sweet Adair
    Marks

1916
(ASCAP)

Allah's Holiday (Friml)
    G. Schirmer, Inc.
Arrah Go On, I'm Gonna Go Back to Oregon
    Mills Music, Inc.
Baby Shoes
    Shapiro, Bernstein & Co., Inc.
Down Among the Sheltering Palms
    Leo Feist, Inc.
Good-Bye, Good Luck, God Bless You
    M. Witmark & Sons
I Ain't Got Nobody
    Leo Feist, Inc.
I Can Dance With Everybody But My Wife
    Harms, Inc.
*Ireland Must Be Heaven for My Mother Came
  From There*
    Leo Feist, Inc.
M-I-S-S-I-S-S-I-P-P-I
    Leo Feist, Inc.
Naughty, Naughty, Naughty
    Shapiro, Bernstein & Co., Inc.
Nola
    Sam Fox Pub. Co.
Poor Butterfly
    Harms, Inc.
Pretty Baby
    Remick Music Corp.

198

Roses of Picardy
    Chappell & Co., Inc.
*There's a Little Bit of Bad in Every Good Little
  Girl*
    Leo Feist, Inc.
They're Wearing 'Em Higher in Hawaii
    Shapiro, Bernstein & Co., Inc.
*What Do You Want To Make Those Eyes at Me
  For?*
    Leo Feist, Inc.
Yaaka-Hula-Hickey-Dula
    Mills Music, Inc.

1917
(ASCAP)

Back Home Again in Indiana
    Shapiro, Bernstein & Co., Inc.
Bells of St. Mary's
    Chappell & Co., Inc.
Darktown Strutters' Ball
    Leo Feist, Inc.
For Me and My Gal
    Mills Music, Inc.
Good-Bye, Broadway; Hello, France
    Leo Feist, Inc.
*I'm All Bound 'Round With the Mason-Dixon
  Line*
    Mills Music, Inc.
Joan of Arc, They Are Calling You
    Mills Music, Inc.
Over There
    Leo Feist, Inc.
Missouri Waltz
    Forster Music Pub., Inc.
Tiger Rag
    Leo Feist, Inc.
Till the Clouds Roll By (Kern)
    T. B. Harms Co.
They Go Wild, Simply Wild Over Me
    Mills Music, Inc.
Where Do We Go From Here?
    Leo Feist, Inc.
Will You Remember (*Maytime* Romberg)
    G. Schirmer, Inc.

(BMI)

Indianola
It Takes a Long, Tall, Brown-Skin Gal   Marks
Lily of the Valley   Marks
Shim-Me-Sha-Wabble   Marks

1918
(ASCAP)

After You've Gone
    Joe Davis, Inc.
Beautiful Ohio
    Shapiro, Bernstein & Co., Inc.

Dear Old Pal of Mine
    Bregman, Vocco & Conn, Inc.
Everything Is Peaches Down in Georgia
    Leo Feist, Inc.
Hello, Central, Give Me No Man's Land
    Mills Music, Inc.
Hindustan
    Forster Music Pub., Inc.
I'm Always Chasing Rainbows
    Robbins Music Corp.
I'm Sorry I Made You Cry
    Leo Feist, Inc.
Ja-Da
    Leo Feist, Inc.
Just a Baby's Prayer at Twilight
    Mills Music, Inc.
K-K-K-Katy
    Leo Feist, Inc.
Keep Your Head Down, "Fritzie Boy"
    Leo Feist, Inc.
Madelon
    Remick Music Corp.
Oh, Frenchy
    Broadway Music Corp.
Oh, How I Hate To Get Up in the Morning
    ABC Music Corp.
Oh, How I Wish I Could Sleep Until My Daddy
Comes Home
    Mills Music, Inc.
Rock-a-Bye Your Baby With a Dixie Melody
    Mills Music, Inc.
Rose of No Man's Land
    Leo Feist, Inc.
Smiles
    Remick Music, Inc.
Somebody Stole My Gal
    Robbins Music Corp.
Sweet Hawaiian Moonlight
    Mayfair Music Corp.
That Tumble Down Shack in Athlons
    Mills Music, Inc.
Till We Meet Again
    Remick Music Corp.
When You Look in the Heart of a Rose
    Leo Feist, Inc.

(BMI)
Original Dixieland One-Step   Marks

1919
(ASCAP)
Alice Blue Gown
    Leo Feist, Inc.
A Pretty Girl Is Like a Melody
    Irving Berlin, Inc.
Chinese Lullaby
    Fisher

Chong, He Come From Hong Kong
    Leo Feist, Inc.
Dardanella
    Mills Music, Inc.
How Ya Gonna Keep 'Em Down on the Farm?
    Mills Music, Inc.
I Know What It Means To Be Lonesome
    Leo Feist, Inc.
I'm Forever Blowing Bubbles
    Remick Music Corp.
Let the Rest of the World Go By
    M. Witmark & Sons
Love Sends a Little Gift of Roses
    Harms, Inc.
Mammy o' Mine
    Shapiro, Bernstein & Co., Inc.
Mandy
    Irving Berlin, Inc.
My Isle of Golden Dreams
    Remick Music Corp.
Nobody Knows (Nobody Seems To Care)
    Irving Berlin, Inc.
Oh, What a Pal Was Mary
    Mills Music, Inc.
On Miami Shore
    Chappell & Co., Inc.
Royal Garden Blues
    Shapiro, Bernstein & Co., Inc.
Smilin' Through
    M. Whitmark & Sons
Swanee
    Harms, Inc.
World Is Waiting for the Sunrise
    Chappell & Co., Inc.
You'd Be Surprised
    Irving Berlin, Inc.
You're a Million Miles From Nowhere
    Mills Music, Inc.
Your Eyes Have Told Me So
    Remick Music Corp.

(BMI)
Blues My Naughtie Sweetie Gives to Me
    Marks
Wait and See
    Marks
You Didn't Want Me When You Had Me
    Marks

1920
(ASCAP)
Avalon
    Remick Music Corp.
Bright Eyes
    Mills Music, Inc.
Broadway Rose
    Mills Music, Inc.

Daddy, You've Been a Mother To Me
    M. Witmark & Sons
Feather Your Nest
    Leo Feist, Inc.
Hold Me
    Robbins Music Corp.
I Never Knew (I Could Love Anybody)
    Leo Feist, Inc.
I Used To Love You, But It's All Over Now
    Broadway Music Corp.
I'll Be With You in Apple Blossom Time
    Broadway Music Corp.
Japanese Sandman
    Remick Music Corp.
Left All Alone Again Blues
    T. B. Harms
Lena From Palesteena
    Shapiro, Bernstein & Co., Inc.
Look for the Silver Lining (Kern)
    T. B. Harms Co.
Love Nest
    Victoria Pub. Co.
Margie
    Mills Music, Inc.
Old Pal, Why Don't You Answer Me?
    Mills Music, Inc.
Rose of Washington Square
    Shapiro, Bernstein & Co., Inc.
Tell Me Little Gypsy
    Irving Berlin, Inc.
The World Is Waiting for the Sunrise
    Chappell & Co., Inc.
When My Baby Smiles at Me
    Harry Von Tilzer Music Pub. Co.
Whispering
    Miller Music, Inc.
Young Man's Fancy
    Leo Feist, Inc.

(BMI)

Argentines, the Portuguese and the Greeks
    Marks

1921

(ASCAP)

Ain't We Got Fun?
    Remick Music Corp.
All by Myself
    Irving Berlin, Inc.
April Showers
    Harms, Inc.
Dapper Dan
    Broadway Music Corp.
Down in Tennessee
    Leo Feist, Inc.
I Ain't Nobody's Darling
    Skidmore Music Co., Inc.

I'm Just Wild About Harry
    M. Witmark & Sons
I Found a Rose in the Devil's Garden
    Mills Music, Inc.
Kitten on the Keys
    Mills Music, Inc.
Leave Me With a Smile
    Mills Music, Inc.
Ma (He's Making Eyes at Me)
    Mills Music, Inc.
Make Believe (Jack Shilkret)
    Mills Music, Inc.
My Mammy
    Bourne, Inc.
My Man (Fanny Brice)
    Leo Feist, Inc.
Over the Hill
    Exclusive Pub., Inc.
Peggy O'Neill
    Leo Feist, Inc.
Say It With Music
    Irving Berlin, Inc.
Second-Hand Rose
    Shapiro, Bernstein & Co., Inc.
Song of Love ("Blossom Time")
    M. Witmark & Sons
The Sheik
    Mills Music, Inc.
Sweet Lady
    Leo Feist, Inc.
Ten Little Fingers and Ten Little Toes
Tuck Me To Sleep in My Old Tucky Home
    Bourne, Inc.
Wabash Blues
    Irving Berlin, Inc.
Wang-Wang Blues
    Leo Feist, Inc.
Yoo-Hoo
    Remick Music Corp.

(BMI)

Jazz Me Blues
    Marks
Who'll Be the Next One To Cry Over You
    Marks

1922

(ASCAP)

Aggravatin' Papa
    Mills Music, Inc.
Ah! Sweet Mystery of Life (revival)
    M. Witmark & Sons
L'Amour Toujours L'Amour
    Harms, Inc.
Carolina in the Morning
    Remick Music Corp.
Chicago   Remick Music Corp.

China Boy
    Leo Feist, Inc.
Crinoline Days
    Irving Berlin, Inc.
Dancing Fool
    Mills Music, Inc.
Georgette
    Shapiro, Bernstein & Co., Inc.
Georgia
    Leo Feist, Inc.
Hot Lips
    Leo Feist, Inc.
Kiss in the Dark, A
    M. Witmark & Sons
I'll Build a Stairway to Paradise
    Harms, Inc.
Lady of the Evening
    Irving Berlin, Inc.
Lovin' Sam the Sheik of Alabam'
    Alger, Yellen & Bornstein, Inc.
Mister Gallagher and Mr. Shean
    Mills Music, Inc.
My Buddy
    Remick Music Corp.
On the Gin Gin Ginny Shore
    Shapiro, Bernstein & Co., Inc.
Parade of the Wooden Soldiers (revival)
    Edw. B. Marks Music Corp.
Stumbling
    Leo Feist, Inc.
Toot Toot Tootsie
    Leo Feist, Inc.
Way Down Yonder in New Orleans
    Shapiro, Bernstein & Co., Inc.
When Hearts Are Young
    Harms, Inc.
Wonderful One
    Leo Feist, Inc.
        (BMI)
In the Little Red Schoolhouse
    Marks
Parade of the Wooden Soldiers
    Marks

1923
(ASCAP)

Annabelle
    Leo Feist, Inc.
Bambalina (Youmans)
    Harms, Inc.
Barney Google
    Remick Music Corp.
Charleston
    Harms, Inc.
I Cried for You, Now It's Your Turn To Cry
Over Me
    Miller Music, Inc.

I Love You (Little Jesse James)
    Leo Feist, Inc.
It Ain't Gonna Rain No Mo'
    Forster Music Pub., Inc.
Just a Girl That Men Forget
    Mills Music, Inc.
Just for Tonight
    Edward B. Marks Corp.
Last Night on the Back Porch
    Skidmore Music Co., Inc.
Linger a While
    Leo Feist, Inc.
My Sweetie Went Away
    Mills Music, Inc.
No, No, Nora
    Leo Feist, Inc.
Oh, Gee; Oh, Gosh; Oh, Golly I'm in Love
    Mills Music, Inc.
A Smile Will Go a Long, Long Way
    Mills Music, Inc.
Swingin' Down the Lane
    Leo Feist, Inc.
That Old Gang of Mine
    Bourne, Inc.
Who's Sorry Now?
    Mills Music, Inc.
Yes, We Have No Bananas
    Skidmore Music Co., Inc.
You Gotta See Mama Every Night
    Leo Feist, Inc.

(BMI)

There'll Be Some Changes Made
    Marks

1924
(ASCAP)

All Alone (Berlin)
    Irving Berlin, Inc.
California, Here I Come
    M. Witmark & Sons
Charley, My Boy
    Bourne, Inc.
Deep in My Heart, Dear
    Harms, Inc.
Everybody Loves M Baby
    Clarence Williams Music Pub. Co., Inc.
Fascinating Rhythm
    Harms, Inc.
I'll See You in My Dreams
    Leo Feist, Inc.
Indian Love Call (Friml)
    Harms, Inc.
I Want To Be Happy
    Harms, Inc.
I Wonder What's Become of Sally
    Ager, Yellen & Bornstein, Inc.

It Had To Be You
    Remick Music Corp.
Jealous
    Mills Music, Inc.
June Night
    Leo Feist, Inc.
Memory Lane
    Harms, Inc.
My Best Girl
    Remick Music Corp.
Nobody's Sweetheart Now
    Mills Music, Inc.
Oh, Katharina
    Leo Feist, Inc.
Rhapsody in Blue (Gershwin)
    Harms, Inc.
Serenade (Student Prince)
    Harms, Inc.
Shine
    Shapiro, Bernstein & Co., Inc.
Somebody Loves Me
    Harms, Inc.
Tea for Two (Youmans)
    Harms, Inc.
What'll I Do?
    Irving Berlin, Inc.
Why Did I Kiss That Girl?
    Shapiro, Bernstein & Co., Inc.

1925
(ASCAP)

Alabamy Bound
    Shapiro, Bernstein & Co., Inc.
Always
    Irving Berlin, Inc.
Away Down South in Heaven
    Shapiro, Bernstein & Co., Inc.
Bam, Bam, Bammy Shore
    Remick Music Corp.
Because I Love You
    Irving Berlin, Inc.
Brown Eyes, Why Are You Blue?
    Mills Music, Inc.
Cecilia
    Irving Berlin, Inc.
Collegiate
    Shapiro, Bernstein & Co., Inc.
A Cup of Coffee, a Sandwich and You
    Harms, Inc.
Dinah
    Mills Music, Inc.
Don't Bring Lulu
    Remick Music Corp.
Drifting and Dreaming
    L. B. Curtis Music Pub.
Five Foot Two, Eyes of Blue
    Leo Feist, Inc.

I Love My Baby
    Shapiro, Bernstein & Co., Inc.
If You Knew Susie
    Shapiro, Bernstein & Co., Inc.
I'm Sitting on Top of the World
    Leo Feist, Inc.
Just a Cottage Small
    Harms, Inc.
Moonlight and Roses
    Villa Moret, Inc.
Oh! How I Miss You Tonight
    Bourne, Inc.
Only a Rose
    Famous Music Corp.
Pal of My Cradle Days
    Leo Feist, Inc.
Prisoner's Song
    Shapiro, Bernstein & Co., Inc.
Rose Marie (Friml)
    Harms, Inc.
Show Me the Way To Go Home
    Harms, Inc.
Sometimes I'm Happy (Youmans)
    Harms, Inc.
Song of the Vagabonds
    Famous Music Corp.
That Certain Feeling
    Harms, Inc.
That Certain Party
    Bourne, Inc.
Ukulele Lady
    Bourne, Inc.
Valencia
    Harms, Inc.
Who (Kern)
    T. B. Harms, Co.
Yes, Sir: That's My Baby
    Bourne, Inc.
(BMI)
Montmartre Rose
    Marks

1926
(ASCAP)

After I Say I'm Sorry
    Leo Feist, Inc.
All Alone Monday
    Harms, Inc.
Baby Face
    Remick Music Corp.
Birth of the Blues
    Harms, Inc.
Black Bottom   Harms, Inc.
Blue Room
    Harms, Inc.
Breezin' Along With the Breeze
    Remick Music Corp.

Bye, Bye, Blackbird
  Remick Music Corp.
Crazy Words (Vo-Do-De-O-Do)
  Advanced Music
Desert Song
  Harms, Inc.
Gimmie a Little Kiss, Will Ya, Huh?
  Irving Berlin, Inc.
Girl Friend, The
  Harms, Inc.
Horses
  Leo Feist, Inc.
I Know That You Know
  Harms, Inc.
Let a Smile Be Your Umbrella
  Mills Music, Inc.
The Little White House at the End of Honeymoon
  Lane
  Shapiro, Bernstein & Co., Inc.
Lonesome and Sorry
  Mills Music, Inc.
Lucky Day
  Harms, Inc.
Moonlight on the Ganges
  Harms, Inc.
My Little Nest of Heavenly Blue
  Edward B. Marks Corp.
One Alone
  Harms, Inc.
The Ranger's Song
  Harms, Inc.
Remember
  Irving Berlin, Inc.
The Rift Song
  Harms, Inc.
Sweet Georgia Brown
  Remick Music Corp.
Tonight You Belong to Me
  Mills Music, Inc.
When Day Is Done
  Harms, Inc.
When the Red, Red Robbin' Comes Bob-Bob-
  Bobbin' Along
  Bourne, Inc.
Where Do You Work-A John?
  Shapiro, Bernstein & Co., Inc.

1927
(ASCAP)

Ain't She Sweet
  Ager, Yellen & Bornstein, Inc.
Among My Souvenirs
  Crawford Music Corp.
At Sundown
  Leo Feist, Inc.
The Best Things in Life Are Free
  Crawford Music Corp.

Blue Skies
  Irving Berlin, Inc.
Can't Help Lovin' Dat Man (Kern)
  T. B. Harms Co.
Charmaine
  Miller Music, Inc.
Chloe
  Villa Moret, Inc.
The Doll Dance
  Miller Music, Inc.
Down South
  Edwards B. Marks Corp.
Girl of My Dreams
  Mills Music, Inc.
Hallelujah (Youmans)
  Harms, Inc.
Here Comes the Showboat
  Shapiro, Bernstein & Co., Inc.
I'm Looking Over a Four-Leaf Clover
  Remick Music Corp.
Just a Memory
  Harms, Inc.
Make Believe (Kern)
  T. B. Harms Co.
Me and My Shadow
  Bourne, Inc.
Melancholy Baby (revival)
  Shapiro, Bernstein & Co., Inc.
Miss Annabelle Lee
  Bourne, Inc.
Muddy Waters
  Boradway Music Corp.
My Blue Heaven
  Leo Feist, Inc.
My Heart Stood Still
  Harms, Inc.
Old Man River (Kern)
  T. B. Harms Co.
Rain
  M. Witmark & Sons
Ramona
  Leo Feist, Inc.
Russian Lullaby
  Irving Berlin, Inc.
Sam, the Old Accordian Man
  Leo Feist, Inc.
Side by Side
  Shapiro, Bernstein & Co., Inc.
Sometimes I'm Happy
  Harms, Inc.
S'Wonderful
  New World Music Corp.
Thou Swell
  Harms, Inc.
Together
  Crawford Music Corp.

The Varsity Drag
Crawford Music Corp.
What Do We Do on a Dew Dew Dewy Day?
Bourne, Inc.
Why Do I Love You?
Harms, Inc.

1928

(ASCAP)

Angelia Mia
Crawford Music Corp.
Button Up Your Overcoat
Crawford Music Corp.
Carolina Moon
Edwin H. Morris & Co., Inc.
C-o-n-s-t-a-n-t-i-n-o-p-l-e
Crawford Music Corp.
Diane
Rubank, Inc.
Diga Diga Doo
Mills Music, Inc.
Don't Hold Everything
Crawford Music Corp.
Get Out and Get Under the Moon
Bourne, Inc.
Honey
Leo Feist, Inc.
I Can't Give You Anything But Love, Baby
Mills Music, Inc.
I Kiss Your Hand, Madame
Harms, Inc.
I Wanna Be Loved by You
Harms, Inc.
I'll Get By
Bourne, Inc.
I'm Bringing a Red, Red Rose
Donaldson, Douglas & Gumble, Inc.
Jeannine, I Dream of Lilac Time
Leo Feist, Inc.
Just Like a Melody Out of the Sky
Donaldson, Douglas & Gumble, Inc.
Let's Do It
Harms, Inc.
Lover, Come Back to Me (Romberg)
Harms, Inc.
Moonlight and Roses
Villa Moret, Inc.
My Lucky Star
Crawford Music Corp.
Precious Little Thing Called Love
Remick Music Corp.
Rio Rita
Leo Feist, Inc.
Softly as in a Morning Sunrise
Harms, Inc.
Sonny Boy
Crawford Music Corp.

Sweet Sue
Shapiro, Bernstein & Co., Inc.
Sweetheart of Sigma Chi (original—1910)
Melrose Music Co., Inc.
Sweethearts on Parade
Joe Davis, Inc.
That's My Weakness Now
Shapiro, Bernstein & Co., Inc.
There's a Rainbow Round My Shoulder
Bourne, Inc.
When You're Smiling
Mills Music, Inc.
You Took Advantage of Me
Harms, Inc.
You're the Cream in My Coffee
Crawford Music Corp.

(BMI)

Marcheta
Cole

1929

(ASCAP)

Ain't Misbehavin'
Miller Music, Inc.
A Little Kiss Each Morning
Harms, Inc.
Am I Blue
M. Witmark & Sons
Aren't We All
Crawford Music Corp.
Can't We Be Friends
Harms, Inc.
Deep Night
Ager, Yellen & Bornstein, Inc.
Great Day
Miller Music, Inc.
Happy Days Are Here Again
Ager, Yellen & Bornstein, Inc.
I'll See You Again
Harms, Inc.
I'll Always Be in Love With You
Shapiro, Bernstein & Co., Inc.
I'm Just a Vagabond Lover
Leo Feist, Inc.
I've Got a Feeling I'm Falling
Santly-Joy-Select, Inc.
Louise
Rubank, Inc.
Moanin' Low
Harms, Inc.
More Than You Know
Mills Music, Inc.
Pagan Love Song
Robbins Music Corp.
Should I
Robbins Music Corp.

Siboney
    Leo Feist, Inc.
Singin' in the Rain
    Robbins Music Corp.
Sunny Side Up
    Crawford Music Corp.
There's Danger in Your Eyes, Cherie
    Bourne, Inc.
Tip Toe Thru the Tulips With Me
    M. Witmark & Sons
They Cut Down the Old Pine Tree
    Miller Music, Inc.
Wedding Bells Are Breaking Up That Old Gang of Mine
    Mills Music, Inc.
Wedding of the Painted Doll
    Sherman, Clay & Co.
When the Organ Played at Twilight
    Santly-Joy Select, Inc.
When It's Springtime in the Rockies
    Villa Moret, Inc.
Why (from *Sons o' Guns*)
    Words & Music, Inc.
Without a Song (Youmans)
    Miller Music, Inc.
Why Was I Born?
    T. B. Harms Co.
You Do Something to Me
    Harms, Inc.
Zigeuner (from *Bitter Sweet*)
    Harms, Inc.

(BMI)

Song of the Islands   Marks

1930

(ASCAP)

Beyond the Blue Horizon
    Famous Music Corp.
Betty Co-Ed
    Carl Fischer, Inc.
Bidin' My Time
    New World Music Corp.
Body and Soul
    Harms, Inc.
Blue Again
    Robbins Music Corp.
Cheerful Little Earful
    Remick Music Corp.
Cryin' for the Carolines
    Remick Music Corp.
Dancing With Tears in My Eyes
    M. Witmark & Sons
Down the River of Golden Dreams
    Leo Feist, Inc.
Embraceable You
    New World Music Corp.

Exactly Like You
    Shapiro, Bernstein & Co., Inc.
I'm Yours
    Remick Music Corp.
I Got Rhythm (Gershwin)
    New World Music Corp.
It Happened in Monterey
    Leo Feist, Inc.
Lady, Play Your Mandolin
    Harms, Inc.
Little White Lies
    Donaldson, Douglas & Gumble, Inc.
Maine Stein Song
    Carl Fischer, Inc.
My Ideal
    Famous Music Corp.
Moonlight on the Colorado
    Shapiro, Bernstein & Co., Inc.
On the Sunny Side of the Street
    Shapiro, Bernstein & Co., Inc.
Sing Something Simple
    Harms, Inc.
Something To Remember You By
    Harms, Inc.
Sweet and Hot
    Ager, Yellen & Bornstein, Inc.
Three Little Words
    Harms, Inc.
Two Hearts in Three-Quarter Time
    Harms, Inc.
Walkin' My Baby Back Home
    Crawford Music Corp.
What Is This Thing Called Love?
    Harms, Inc.
Would You Like To Take a Walk
    Remick Music Corp.
You're Driving Me Crazy
    Donaldson, Douglas & Gumble, Inc.
You Brought a New Kind of Love to Me
    Famous Music Corp.

(BMI)

Mama Inez
    Marks
Peanut Vendor
    Marks

1931

(ASCAP)

All of Me
    Bourne, Inc.
Auf Wiedersehen
    Ager, Yellen & Bornstein, Inc.
Cuban Love Song
    Robbins Music, Inc.
Dancing in the Dark
    Harms, Inc.

205

Drums in My Heart
    Miller Music, Inc.
Good Night, Sweetheart
    M. Witmark & Sons
Guilty
    Leo Feist, Inc.
I Found a Million Dollar Baby in a Five and
    Ten-Cent Store
    Remick Music Corp.
I Love a Parade
    Harms, Inc.
I Surrender, Dear
    Mills Music, Inc.
Life Is Just a Bowl of Cherries
    Crawford Music Corp.
Moonlight Saving Time
    Leo Feist, Inc.
Out of Nowhere
    Famous Music Corp.
River, Stay 'Way From My Door
    Shapiro, Bernstein & Co., Inc.
Sleepy Time Down South
    Mills Music, Inc.
Smile, Darn Ya', Smile
    Crawford Music Corp.
Someday I'll Find You
    Harms, Inc.
Sweet and Lovely
    Robbins Music Corp.
That's Why Darkies Were Born
    Crawford Music Corp.
This Is the Mrs.
    Crawford Music Corp.
Time on My Hands
    Miller Music, Inc.
Wabash Moon
    Bourne, Inc.
The Waltz You Saved for Me
    Leo Feist, Inc.
When I Take My Sugar to Tea
    Famous Music Corp.
When the Moon Comes Over the Mountain
    Robbins Music Corp.
When We're Alone (Penthouse Serenade)
    Famous Music Corp.
When Your Hair Has Turned to Silver
    Joe Morris Co.
When Yuba Plays the Rumba on the Tuba
    Harms, Inc.
Where the Blue of the Night Meets the Gold of the
    Day
    Crawford Music Corp.
You're My Everything
    Harms, Inc.

(BMI)

Marta   Marks

206

Mama Don't Want No Peas an' Rice an' Cocoanut
Oil
    Marks

1932
(ASCAP)

April in Paris
    Harms, Inc.
Brother, Can You Spare a D'me
    Harms, Inc.
Forty-Second Street
    M. Witmark & Sons
How Deep Is the Ocean?
    Irving Berlin, Inc.
I've Told Every Little Star
    T. B. Harms, Inc.
Just an Echo in the Valley
    Robbins Music Corp.
Let's Put Out the Light and Go To Sleep
    Harms, Inc.
Little Street Where Old Friends Meet
    Joe Morris Music Co.
Louisiana Hayride
    Harms, Inc.
Lullaby of the Leaves
    Bourne, Inc.
Masquerade
    Leo Feist, Inc.
Night and Day
    Harms, Inc.
Paradise (waltz)
    Mills Music, Inc.
Say It Isn't So
    Irving Berlin, Inc.
A Shanty in Old Shantytown
    M. Witmark & Sons
Shuffle Off to Buffalo
    M. Witmark & Sons
Snuggle on Your Shoulder
    Leo Feist, Inc.
Somebody Loves You
    Joe Morris Music Co.
Too Many Tears
    M. Witmark & Sons
You're an Old Smoothie
    Harms, Inc.

(BMI)

Georgia on My Mind
    Peer

1933
(ASCAP)

Annie Doesn't Live Here Any More
    Bourne, Inc.
Boulevard of Broken Dreams
    Remick Music Corp.
By a Waterfall   M. Witmark & Sons

Carioca
T. B. Harms Co.
Did You Ever See a Dream Walking?
Crawford Music Corp.
Don't Blame Me
Robbins Music Corp.
Easter Parade
Irving Berlin, Inc.
Fit As a Fiddle
Leo Feist, Inc.
Flying Down to Rio
T. B. Harms Co.
Have You Ever Been Lonely?
Shapiro, Bernstein & Co., Inc.
I Cover the Waterfront
Harms, Inc.
In the Valley of the Moon
Joe Morris Music Co.
Last Round-Up
Shapiro, Bernstein & Co., Inc.
Lazy Bones
Southern Music Pub. Co., Inc.
Let's Fall in Love
Bourne, Inc.
Love Is the Sweetest Thing
Harms, Inc.
Lover
Famous Music Corp.
My Moonlight Madonna
Carl Fischer, Inc.
Orchids in the Moonlight
T. B. Harms Co.
Shadow Waltz
Remick Music Corp.
Smoke Gets in Your Eyes
T. B. Harms Co.
Sophisticated Lady
Mills Music, Inc.
Stars Fell on Alabama
Mills Music, Inc.
Stormy Weather
Mills Music, Inc.
Talk of the Town
Leo Feist, Inc.
The Gold Diggers Song, We're in the Money
Remick Music Corp.
The Touch of Your Hands
T. B. Harms Co.
Two Tickets to Georgia
Bourne, Inc.
Underneath the Harlem Moon
Crawford Music Corp.
We Just Couldn't Say Goodbye
Words & Music, Inc.
Who's Afraid of the Big Bad Wolf
Bourne, Inc.

(BMI)

Lazy River
Peer
Play, Fiddle, Play
Marks

1934

(ASCAP)

All I Do Is Dream of You
Robbins Music Corp., Inc.
Anything Goes   Harms, Inc.
Be Still My Heart
Broadway Music Corp.
The Beat o' My Heart
Bourne, Inc.
Cocktails for Two
Famous Music Corp.
The Continental
Harms, Inc.
Everything I Have Is Yours
Robbins Music Corp.
Hands Across the Table
Mills Music, Inc.
I Get a Kick Out of You
Harms, Inc.
I Only Have Eyes for You
Remick Music Corp.
I Saw Stars
Robbins Music Corp.
I'll Follow My Secret Heart
Chappell & Co., Inc.
I'll String Along With You
M. Witmark & Sons
Isle of Capri
T. B. Harms Co.
June in January
Famous Music Corp.
Little Man, You've Had a Busy Day
T. B. Harms Co.
Love in Bloom
Famous Music Corp.
Love Thy Neighbor
Crawford Music Corp.
My Little Grass Shack in Kealakekua
Sherman, Clay & Co.
No, No, a Thousand Times No
Leo Feist, Inc.
The Object of My Affections
Bourne, Inc.
Old Spinning Wheel
Shapiro, Bernstein & Co., Inc.
Santa Claus Is Coming to Town
Leo Feist, Inc.
Solitude
Exclusive Pub., Inc.
Stay as Sweet as You Are

207

Crawford Music Corp.

There Goes My Heart
　　Leo Feist, Inc.

Two Cigarettes in the Dark
　　Crawford Music Corp.

Wagon Wheels
　　Shapiro, Bernstein & Co., Inc.

Winter Wonderland
　　Bregman, Vocco & Conn, Inc.

With My Eyes Wide Open I'm Dreaming
　　Crawford Music Corp.

You and the Night and the Music
　　Harms, Inc.

You're the Top
　　Harms, Inc.

You Oughta Be in Pictures
　　Harms, Inc.

1935
(ASCAP)

Alone
　　Robbins Music Corp.

Beautiful Lady in Blue
　　Chappell & Co., Inc.

Begin the Beguine
　　Harms, Inc.

Bess, You Is My Woman
　　Gershwin Pub. Corp.

Broadway Rhythm
　　Robbins Music Corp.

Cheek to Cheek
　　Irving Berlin, Inc.

Deep Purple
　　Robbins Music Corp.

I'm Gonna Sit Right Down and Write Myself a Letter
　　Crawford Music Corp.

I'm in the Mood for Love
　　Robbins Music Corp.

I Got Plenty of Nuttin
　　Gershwin Pub. Corp.

In a Little Gypsy Tea Room
　　Edwin H. Morris & Co., Inc.

It Ain't Necessarily So
　　Gershwin Pub. Corp.

Just One of Those Things
　　Harms, Inc.

Lovely to Look At
　　T. B. Harms Co.

Lullaby of Broadway
　　M. Witmark & Sons

Maybe
　　Rialto Music Pub. Co.

Music Goes Round and Round
　　Santly-Joy-Select, Inc.

My Romance
　　T. B. Harms Co.

208

On the Good Ship Lollipop
　　Movietone Music Corp.

On Treasure Island
　　Joe Morris Music Co.

Red Sails in the Sunset
　　Shapiro, Bernstein & Co., Inc.

Roll Along, Prairie Moon
　　Robbins Music Corp.

Stardust
　　Mills Music, Inc.

Tell Me That You Love Me Tonight
　　T. B. Harms Co.

Thanks a Million
　　Robbins Music Corp.

Top Hat, White Tie and Tails
　　Irving Berlin, Inc.

When I Grow Too Old To Dream
　　Robbins Music Corp.

You Are My Lucky Star
　　Robbins Music Corp.

1936
(ASCAP)

DeLovely　　　　　　Chappell & Co., Inc.

Empty Saddles
　　Shapiro, Bernstein & Co., Inc.

Goody Goody
　　Crawford Music Corp.

I'm an Old Cowhand
　　Leo Feist, Inc.

In the Chapel in the Moonlight
　　Shapiro, Bernstein & Co., Inc.

Is It True What They Say About Dixie?
　　Irving Caesar

It's a Sin To Tell a Lie
　　Bregman, Vocco & Conn, Inc.

I've Got You Under My Skin
　　Chappell & Co., Inc.

Lights Out
　　Shapiro, Bernstein & Co., Inc.

Melody From the Sky
　　Famous Music Corp.

Moon Over Miami
　　Bourne, Inc.

Music Goes 'Round and 'Round
　　Santly-Joy-Select, Inc.

These Foolish Things Remind Me of You
　　Bourne, Inc.

The Way You Look Tonight
　　Chappell & Co., Inc.

When Did You Leave Heaven?
　　Robbins Music Corp.

You Turned the Tables on Me
　　Movietone Music Corp.
(BMI)

Say Si Si
　　Marks

1937
(ASCAP)

Boo Hoo
Shapiro, Bernstein & Co., Inc.
I'd Be Lost Without You
Leo Feist, Inc.
In the Still of the Night
Chappell & Co., Inc.
Little Old Lady
Chappell & Co., Inc.
The One Rose (That's Left in My Heart)
Shapiro, Bernstein & Co., Inc.
Rosalie
Chappell & Co., Inc.
Sweet Leilani
Santly-Joy-Select, Inc.
Thanks for the Memory
Paramount Music Corp.
That Old Feeling
Leo Feist, Inc.
When My Dreamboat Comes Home
M. Witmark & Sons
Where or When
Chappell & Co., Inc.

1938
(ASCAP)

A-Tisket A-Tasket
Robbins Music Corp.
Bei Mir Bist Du Schoen
Harms, Inc.
Cathedral in the Pines
Bourne, Inc.
Flat Foot Floogee
Green Bros. & Knight, Inc.
Heigh Ho
Bourne, Inc.
I've Got a Pocketful of Dreams
Santly-Joy-Select, Inc.
Love Walked In
Gershwin Pub. Corp.
Music, Maestro, Please
Bourne, Inc.
Says My Heart
Famous Music Corp.
September Song
Crawford Music Corp.
There's a Gold Mine in the Sky
Bourne, Inc.
Umbrella Man
Harms, Inc.
Whistle While You Work
Bourne, Inc.
(BMI)
Mexicali Rose
Cole

1939
(ASCAP)

All the Things You Are
Chappell & Co., Inc.
At the Balalaika (pub. in Eng. 1936)
Leo Feist, Inc.
Beer Barrel Polka
Shapiro, Bernstein & Co., Inc.
Begin the Beguine
Harms, Inc.
Deep Purple
Robbins Music Co.
Do I Love You?
Chappell & Co., Inc.
Jeepers Creepers
H. Witmark & Sons
Moon Love
Famous Music Corp.
Over the Rainbow
Leo Feist, Inc.
Penny Serenade
Shapiro, Bernstein & Co., Inc.
Scatterbrain
Bregman, Vocco & Conn, Inc.
South of the Border
Shapiro, Bernstein & Co., Inc.
Sunrise Serenade
Jewel Music Pub. Co., Inc.
Three Little Fishes
Santly-Joy-Select, Inc.
Very Thought of You
M. Witmark & Sons
Wishing
G. Schirmer, Inc.
You Must Have Been a Beautiful Baby
Remick Music Corp.

(BMI)

Adios, Marquita Linda
Peer
El Rancho Grande
Marks
Jumpin' Jive
Marks

1940
(ASCAP)

Careless
Bourne, Inc.
Ferryboat Serenade
Robbins Music Corp.
God Bless America
Irving Berlin, Inc.
I'll Never Smile Again
Sun Music Co., Inc.
In an Old Dutch Garden
Harms, Inc.

Let's Be Buddies
    Chappell & Co., Inc.
Oh Johnny, Oh Johnny, Oh!
    Forster Music Pub. Co.
Only Forever
    Santly-Joy-Select, Inc.
When You Wish Upon a Star
    Bourne, Inc.
        (BMI)
Do I Worry
    Melody Lane
Frenesi
    Peer
I Hear a Rhapsody
    BMI
Just a Little Bit South of North Carolina
    Porgie
Practice Makes Perfect
    BMI
Strange Fruit
    Marks
The Breeze and I
    Marks
Tango of Roses
    Marks
Walkin' by the River
    BMI
We Could Make Such Beautiful Music
    BMI
You Walk By
    BMI

1941
(ASCAP)
Anniversary Waltz
    Carl Fischer, Inc.
Chattanooga Choo Choo
    Leo Feist, Inc.
Cherry
    Peer
He Wears a Pair of Silver Wings
    Shapiro, Bernstein & Co., Inc.
        (BMI)
Amapola
    Marks
Bababu
    Peer
Daddy
    Republic
Deep in the Heart of Texas
    Melody Lane
G'Bye Now
    BMI
Green Eyes
    Peer
He's 1-A in the Army   Marks

210

High on a Windy Hill
    BMI
Hut Sut Song
    Schumann
I Don't Want To Set the World on Fire
    Cherio
It All Comes Back to Me Now
    BMI
My Sister and I
    BMI
So You're the One
    BMI
There'll Be Some Changes Made (1923)
    Marks
Yours
    Marks

1942
(ASCAP)
Army Air Corps Song
    Carl Fischer, Inc.
Don't Sit Under the Apple Tree
    Robbins Music Corp.
He's a Right Guy
    Chappell & Co., Inc.
Johnny Doughboy
    Crawford Music Corp.
Jingle Jangle Jingle
    Paramount Music Corp.
Moonlight Cocktails
    Jewel Music Pub. Co., Inc.
Praise the Lord and Pass the Ammunition
    Famous Music Corp.
Rose O'Day
    Tobias-Lewis
There's a Star Spangled Banner Waving
    Bob Miller, Inc.
There'll be Blue Birds Over the White Cliffs of
    Dover
        Shapiro, Bernstein & Co., Inc.
This Is the Army, Mr. Jones
    Irving Berlin Music Co.
Warsaw Concerto
    Chappell & Co., Inc.
When the Lights Go On Again All Over the World
    Campbell-Porgie
White Christmas
    Irving Berlin, Inc.
        (BMI)
Remember Pearl Harbor
    Republic
Tonight We Love
    Maestro
Yours
    Marks

1943

All or Nothing At All
　Leeds Music Corp.
As Time Goes By
　Harms, Inc.
By the River of the Roses
　Shapiro, Bernstein & Co., Inc.
Comin' In on a Wing and a Prayer
　Robbins Music Corp.
Don't Get Around Much Anymore
　Robbins Music Corp.
I Had the Craziest Dream
　Bregman, Vocco & Conn, Inc.
In the Blue of Evening
　Shapiro, Bernstein & Co., Inc.
I've Heard That Song Before
　E. H. Morris & Co., Inc.
Let's Get Lost
　Paramount Music Corp.
Moonlight Becomes You
　Famous Music Corp.
My Heart Tells Me
　Bregman, Vocco & Conn, Inc.
Oh, What a Beautiful Morning
　Crawford Music Corp.
People Will Way We're in Love
　Crawford Music Corp.
Speak Low
　Chappell & Co., Inc.
Sunday, Monday or Always
　Mayfair Music Corp.
Surrey With the Fringe on Top
　Williamson, Inc.
That Old Black Magic
　Famous Music Corp.
There Are Such Things
　Yankee
They're Either Too Young or Too Old
　M. Witmark & Sons
You'd Be So Nice To Come Home To
　Chappell & Co., Inc.
You'll Never Know
　Bregman, Vocco & Conn, Inc.

(BMI)

Besame Mucho
　Peer
Brazil
　Peer
Paper Doll
　Marks
Pistol Packing Mama
　Dexter
When the Lights Go On Again
　Porgie

1944

Bell Bottom Trousers
　Santly-Joy-Select, Inc.
Don't Fence Me In
　Harms, Inc.
Goodnight Wherever You Are
　Shapiro, Bernstein & Co., Inc.
Holiday For Strings
　Bregman, Vocco & Conn, Inc.
I Love You (Porter)
　Chappell & Co., Inc.
I'll Be Seeing You
　Harms, Inc.
I'll Walk Alone
　Edwin B. Morris & Co., Inc.
It's Love, Love, Love
　Santly-Joy-Select, Inc.
Mairzy Doats
　Miller Music, Inc.
San Fernando Valley
　Mayfair Music Corp.
Shoo Shoo Baby
　Leeds Music Corp.
Swinging On a Star
　Burke Van Heusen
Trolley Song
　Leo Feist, Inc.

(BMI)

Amor
　Peer
Poinciana
　Marks
Tico Tico
　Peer
What a Difference a Day Made (1934)
　Marks

1945

(ASCAP)

Ac-Cent-Tchu-Ate the Positive
　Edw. H. Morris & Co.
All of My Life
　Mills Music, Inc.
Candy
　Leo Feist, Inc.
Don't Fence Me In
　Harms, Inc.
Dream
　Capitol
If I Loved You
　Williamson Music, Inc.
Isn't It Kinda Fun
　Williamson Music, Inc.
It's Been a Long, Long Time
　Edwin H. Morris & Co.

It's a Grand Night for Singing   Williamson
June Is Bustin' Out All Over   Williamson
Laura   Robbins
Little on the Lonely Side (A)   Advanced
My Dreams Are Getting Better All the Time
     Santly-Joy
On the Atchison, Topeka and the Santa Fe   Feist
Saturday Night Is the Lonliest Night in the Week
Sentimental Journey   Morris
That's for Me   Williamson
Till the End of Time   Santly-Joy

(BMI)

Bata   Peer
My Heart Sings   France
There, I've Said It Again   Valiant
There Must Be a Way   Stevens
Twilight Time   Porgie
Waitin' for the Train To Come In   Block
You Belong to My Heart   Peer

1946
(ASCAP)

Day by Day   Barton
Doin' What Comes Naturally   Berlin
Five Minutes More   Melrose
Girl That I Marry   Irving Berlin
Gypsy (The)   Leeds Music Corp.
I Can't Begin To Tell You   Bregmann
I Got the Sun in the Morning   Irving Berlin
It Might as Well Be Spring   Williamson
Let It Snow, Let It Snow, Let It Snow
     Edwin H. Morris & Co., Inc.
Oh, What It Seemed To Be   Santly-Joy, Inc.
Ole Buttermilk Sky   Burke & Van Heusen
Old Lamplighter Song   ??
Personality   Burke & Van Heusen
Shoo Fly Pie and Apple Pan Dowdy   Capitol
Sioux City Sue   Morris
South America, Take It Away   Witmark
Symphony   Chappell & Co., Inc.
They Say It's Wonderful   Irving Berlin
To Each His Own   Paramount

(BMI)

Atlanta, G. A.   Stevens
Laughing on the Outside   BMI
The Coffee Song   Valiant

1947
(ASCAP)

Anniversary Song   Mood Music
Dream, Dream, Dream   John Thomas
The Egg and I   Miller Music Corp.
A Gal in Calico   Remick
How Are Things in Glocca Morra   Players
I Tipped My Hat and Slowly Rode Away
     Robbins Music Corp.

It's a Good Day   Capitol Songs
Linda   (1945) Leeds
Mam'selle   Leo Feist, Inc.
Zip a Dee Do Dah   Santy-Joy, Inc.

(BMI)

Managua, Nicaragua   Encore
Misirlou   Colonial
My Adobe Hacienda   Peer
Open the Door, Richard   Duchess
Smoke, Smoke, Smoke   American
A, Your Adorable
There'll Be Some Changes Made (1922)
     Marks

1948
(ASCAP)

Ballerina   Jefferson Music Co.
Beg Your Pardon   Robbins Music Corp.
But Beautiful   Famous Music Corp.
Buttons and Bows   Famous Music Corp.
Civilization   Edwin H. Morris & Co., Inc.
Far Away Places   Laurel Music Corp.
Golden Earrings   Famous Music Corp.
I'll Dance at Your Wedding   George Simon, Inc.
It's Magic   M. Witmark & Sons
Manana   Barbour-Lee
My Darling, My Darling   Ed Morris
My Happiness   Blasco
Nature Boy   Morris
Near You
     Bregman, Vocco & Conn, Inc.
Now Is the Hour   Leeds Music Corp.
On a Slow Boat to China   Morris
Powder Your Face With Sunshine
     Bregman, Vocco & Conn, Inc.
Serenade of the Bells   Melrose
Tree in the Meadow   Shapiro, Bernstein
You Call Everybody Darlin'   Mayfair
You Were Only Foolin'   Shapiro, Bernstein

(BMI)

Hair of Gold, Eyes of Blue   Mellin
Bouquet of Roses   Hill & Range

1949
(ASCAP)

Cruising Down the River   Spilter
Forever and Ever   Robbins
Careless Hands   Melrose
Red Roses for a Blue Lady   Mills
"A" You're Adorable   Laurel
Sunflower   Famous
Far Away Places   Laurel
So Tored   Glenmore
Again   Robbins
Some Enchanted Evening   Williamson
I'm in Love with a Wonderful Guy   Williamson